AFRICAN SOCIALISM

African Socialism

A BACKGROUND BOOK

Fenner Brockway

DUFOUR EDITIONS
CHESTER SPRINGS
PENNSYLVANIA

To my friends in Africa

Library of Congress Catalog Card Number: 63-21144
Manufactured in Great Britain
First published in the U.S.A. 1963

CONTENTS

I

From European Capitalism to African Socialism

THE African continent of the twentieth century is the child of Europe's industrial revolution in the nineteenth century. The need for raw materials and markets, and later for foodstuffs and profitable investment, led to the scramble for the occupation of Africa which culminated in the partition of the continent at the Berlin Congress of 1885.

There had, of course, been incursions before—for example, the Portuguese occupation of Angola is three centuries old—but the great drive for possession responded to the economic demands arising from the birth and growth of capitalism. This should be in our minds as we begin our survey of the birth and growth of African socialism.

France acquired one-third of Africa, including the territories on the Mediterranean from Tunisia to Morocco, the western bulge of the pear-shaped continent, and far down to the core until it reached the river Congo. Italy stretched across the Mediterranean to Libya and encamped on the east coast in Somalia and Eritrea. Germany took over Tanganyika in the east, Togoland and the Cameroons in the west, and South West Africa. Belgium, or rather King Leopold, became lord of the vast rubber plantations of the Congo. Spain crossed the Straits of Gibraltar to western Morocco and, with Portugal, established enclaves further south on the west coast. Portugal also confirmed by annexation her seventeenth-century penetration into the wide areas of Angola and Mozambique.

The British colonialists spread themselves far over the continent. They dominated Egypt and, with Egypt, the Sudan. They took a large part of east Africa, including Uganda and Kenya and the islands of Zanzibar, and pushed deep into central Africa, Nyasaland and the Rhodesias. They thrust the Dutch settlers inland from the southern toe of Africa at the Cape of Good Hope. In west Africa they took over the vast area of Nigeria, Sierra Leone, the Gold Coast (now Ghana) and Gambia. In all, one-third of the territory, and one-fourth of the population, of the British Empire were added during the last thirty years of the nineteenth century.

Whilst the first urges from the factories of the industrial revolution were for raw materials and markets, these did not prove nearly so profitable as the investment of surplus capital. During the second half of the nineteenth century the proportion of imports into Britain from its overseas possessions varied between 20·7 and 28·8 per cent, substantial but not dominating. The market for goods in Africa and other colonial territories was limited by the poverty of the peoples; most of them existed on a subsistence economy without handling cash. But the financiers prospered.

Indeed, in the British areas of east, central and southern Africa the administration in the first instance was conducted not by Whitehall but by chartered profit-making companies. In Uganda the British East Africa Company took charge in 1890, preceding the British Protectorate by four years. In the Rhodesias the British South Africa Company, financial achievement of Cecil Rhodes, was, under a charter in 1889, given supreme powers over three-quarters of a million square miles; it retained this hold in Southern Rhodesia until 1923 and in Northern Rhodesia until 1924.*

* On becoming responsible for the administration, the British and Southern Rhodesian Governments bought out the land rights of the British South Africa Company for £3,750,000, plus a half interest in

The methods by which the companies acquired possession of the territories and their resources would not to-day be regarded as moral. Sir Roy Welensky is a rather surprising witness to this fact. When he moved a resolution on March 24, 1949, in the Northern Rhodesian Legislative Council, calling for a special tax on mining royalties, he referred to the 'shameful story' of how concessions were extracted from the chiefs:

'These agreements, if you can call them that, were negotiated in the early part of the nineties.... You had a company-cum-government which was negotiating with African chiefs. I have no doubt that the company knew what it was after. I certainly question whether the African chief knew that he was disposing of or parting with the mineral rights.'

The most profitable investments in Africa have been in minerals—copper, gold, diamonds, uranium, many others. An economic empire of mining companies was established in central and southern Africa, stretching from the copper belt in Northern Rhodesia across Katanga and Angola to South West Africa and the Rand in South Africa. The companies were closely linked by common directors and shareholdings. In recent years they have yielded fantastic profits of 50, 100 and even 200 per cent.

One of the problems of expanding capitalism in the towns of Africa was the recruitment of labour from the native population whose traditional life was in tribal agricultural communities. This need was met by the eviction of thousands of families from selected territories which were transferred to European possession. The

---

the sales of land for forty years. It was not until 1933 that the mineral rights were bought out; the price, £2 million. In Northern Rhodesia an agreement with the British Government permits the Company to keep its mineral rights until 1986, paying 20 per cent in taxation. In the five years to 1960 the BSA Company pocketed, in round figures, £50 million in mining royalties.

resulting land hunger drove the able-bodied males into the towns. This policy was followed with particular ruthlessness in South Africa and the Rhodesias. In the case of the Rhodesias, the Monckton Commission reported in 1960 that 48 million acres, the size of England and Wales, were allotted to Europeans, whose total population numbered that of a medium-sized town in Britain, while the millions of Africans were restricted to 41 million acres.

In later years the wages paid to African labourers in the mines were a sufficient magnet. The payment was wretchedly low—one-tenth of what was given to the European workers—but this was wealth to the thousands who had existed at subsistence level. Even in colonies like Kenya, where there were no minerals to exploit, the land hunger which followed the occupation of rich farming areas by European settlers compelled Africans to seek work in the towns or on the farms under serf-like conditions.

The map of Africa drawn by the Berlin Congress was arbitrary and artificial, reflecting the territory occupied by companies, traders, soldiers and missionaries and not racial association or geographical separation. The consequence was that tribes and even families were heartlessly divided. The economies of the territories became equally artificial. The first concern of the occupying powers was inevitably the need of their own industries rather than the needs of the indigenous peoples. Seeking raw materials, markets and profitable investment, they paid little regard to establishing balanced economies. In the earlier years there were no cotton mills, no coffee-processing plants, no factories for making chocolate, furniture, boots and shoes or for canning fruit, despite the raw cotton, coffee, cocoa, timber, hide and fruit at hand. There are very few still.

* * *

We shall get a wrong picture of Africa, however, if we regard the effects of British and other colonialisms as entirely regressive. Different powers adopted different political methods. The French and the Portuguese integrated their colonies with their homelands, giving their own nationals and a few African educated élite voting rights for the legislatures in Paris and Lisbon, but denying distinctive nationhood to the peoples; the Belgians withheld political rights from Africans, administering through their civil service. The British, on the other hand, set themselves the goal of colonial self-government, beginning by indirect rule through the chiefs, progressing from nominated to elected African members of the legislatures, and finally to independence.

All three systems were marred by repressions, but the British theory was undoubtedly the most enlightened. More than three-quarters of the population in the former British colonies now enjoy full self-government and independence, and we have not yet had France's unhappy experience of an Algerian war (though at the time of writing there is a danger that it may be partly repeated in Southern Rhodesia) nor the chaos which Belgium left behind in the Congo. Both France and Belgium have finally had to adopt the British goal of independence.

No one can visit African territories without appreciating the material contribution which the European colonisers have made. One sees it in Cairo, Tunis, Algiers, Casablanca, Accra, Lagos, Khartoum, Kampala, Nairobi, Dar-es-Salaam—modern buildings, shops filled with the same articles as in the shops of London, Paris or Berlin, impressive civic headquarters, business offices, garages, hotels, new factories, cars in procession on good roads.

There are two photographs in the biography of Sir Roy Welensky* which illustrate the change. The first is of a stretch of arid land crossed by a muddy ditch, a revolting waste. The second is of a broad boulevard, lined with well-designed modern buildings, a double avenue of tall

* *The Welensky Story* by Garry Allighan (Macdonald, 30s.).

palm trees beautifying its centre. The photographs are of exactly the same site—divided by less than fifty years. Salisbury as it was and is typifies the change which has taken place in towns throughout Africa by the coming of the Europeans.

It is true, of course, that the advantages of this transformation have gone primarily to the Europeans. It is they mostly—but not entirely—who occupy the modern buildings, who buy the refrigerators and fashionable clothes displayed in the shops, and who speed by in the cars. It is true that in the back streets of the same towns the Africans exist in squalid conditions. It is true that the companies which occupy the up-to-date offices are owned by European and American financiers and shareholders who withdraw large revenues from the territories in profit. Nevertheless, here is the material shell of progress which divides primitive Africa from an Africa which has become modern. As Africans surge from these back streets and take possession of the shell and enjoy its fruits, they should remember sometimes that without the Europeans it would not yet have been constructed.

Colonialism similarly gave Africa its first roads and railways, its first dams to distribute electrical power, its pipe-lines and channels of irrigation, its machinery for mines and factories, its modern techniques of soil preservation and agriculture, the ships which serve its ports, the aircraft which touch down at its airports. Admittedly, as in the case of the modernised towns, the motive was sometimes, though not always, to serve primarily the European population and European interests, but even so the Africans have also reaped some of the benefits and are inheriting the basis on which they can build their new states and societies.

Colonialism brought the beginnings of modern education to Africans, inadequate (approximately for 40 per cent of the children), poor compared with the education provided to the children of the white settlers, but, over most of the continent, at least a beginning. Europe gave Africa the first benefits of a modern medical service, again inadequate (often only one doctor to 43,000 people), and European science, with the aid of the United Nations, has conquered malaria over wide areas and is conquering leprosy. The missionary societies contributed much to education and health, and in recent years many of them have stood courageously for African rights.

African students have been helped by the colonialist powers to go to the universities of Europe, and embryonic universities have been established by colonial aid in many parts of Africa itself. From Europe—particularly from the classical writers of Britain and France—have come the philosophy of political freedom and democracy, the model of representative institutions and a legal code, and the conception of an independent and impartial judiciary. Other nations—America, Soviet Russia, Yugoslavia and Israel among them—have in recent years also acted as hosts to African students, sometimes motivated by enlightened charity, sometimes by ideological and strategic purposes.

The liberal ideas of the political philosophers of the nineteenth century have often been denied by the colonial powers in practice. But when we balance the rights and wrongs of colonialism the contribution of its progressive influences—material, human, intellectual and spiritual—must be placed on the credit side. African leaders, beginning their constructive task of nation building with the advantage of the technical achievements of colonialism, themselves often educated in mission schools and European universities, are the first to recognise what they owe to those who took possession of their countries in the nineteeth century, however deeply they resent the fact of the occupation and the repressions and humiliations by which it was retained.

It is important that we should recognise the nature of the New Africa which is now emerging from the European occupation. The New Africa is not only a continent which claims the right to govern itself in political independence, to reflect racial equality in all things and to express proudly the personality of the African peoples. It is concerned not only to end colonialism. What is not so fully realised is that the African leaders and African national movements are to an extraordinary degree dedicated also to the task of repudiating the capitalism whose urges led to the occupation of their continent in the nineteenth century and of consciously directing their new independent states towards the creation of socialist societies. Nearly every politically alert African nationalist regards himself as a socialist. The exceptions are those who hold privileged positions in their own societies—some chiefs, for instance, who have become landed proprietors, business and professional men, administrators who cannot shake off the bureaucratic tradition of the colonialist Establishment. "African nationalists are instinctively socialist", an African leader once remarked in my presence.

Africans resent alien economic control as much as they resent alien political control. They are frustrated by alien ownership of mines, plantations and factories, and by the racial inequality of alien managements, alien skilled craftsmen, alien workers paid more than African workers on similar jobs. They are humiliated by the social superiority and segregation which these privileges involve. They resent the way in which white settlers and financial corporations have taken possession of their best land in many parts of Africa. They regard themselves as living under an economic occupation and identify their economic masters with the colonialism against which they are in revolt. They have been led to socialism by their nationalism.

The trend of Africa towards socialism has been evident ever since Dr Nkrumah became Prime Minister of the Gold Coast, President Nasser nationalised the Suez Canal and M. Sékou Touré headed Guinea to independence from France. But I, for one, did not appreciate the strength of the sweep to socialism until I attended the third All-African Peoples' Conference at Cairo in March, 1961.

It was a conference of the main nationalist movements in Africa except the ex-French colonies of West and Equatorial Africa. President Nasser welcomed us, emphasising the solidarity of the Arab North with Black Africa south of the Sahara, and insisting that the aim of African independence must be economic and cultural as well as political. This was the dominating theme of the conference. It was concerned, of course, with the expansion of African democracy to areas still under white occupation, but the new and main subject of interest was resistance to "neo-colonialism", the economic and cultural domination of the continent by old colonial interests and influences even after nations obtain independence.

The conference was militantly socialist, accepting socialism without dispute as the answer to "neo-colonialism". Some of the delegates leaned towards communism but the great majority were essentially neutralist, unwilling to follow either the communist or the social democratic model, dedicated to establishing African socialism.

The political resolutions were inclined to be demagogic, repetitive and platitudinous, but on the economic side they were more concrete. They proposed the modification of structures in order effectively 'to subordinate the economy of the countries to the needs of national interests' by the nationalisation of the natural resources, the main plantations, banks, insurance companies, transport and foreign-owned industries. Such public ownership, it was urged, 'constitutes the inalienable right of every people and is indispensable condition of their liberty, security and welfare'. They asked for agrarian reforms, national currencies, and the control of exports, imports and investments.

They also had in mind Pan-African aims of continental co-ordination. They called for a committee of experts to prepare a common economic policy for all Africa, including an inter-state African Transport Corporation (land, sea and air), an all-African bank, multilateral customs and foreign exchange agreements, and the creation of a Common African Market. Respect for the democratic rights of trades unions was demanded and (which libertarians will find interesting) 'the creation of a supranational council of states which can control and examine cases involving the violation of the democratic rights of workers'.

Such is the mood of the popular mass-movements of Africa. Perhaps the Cairo Conference was sophisticated, led by almost professional politicians, owing allegiance to definite ideologies. The simple terms of the Freedom Charter, adopted by the Congress of the People in South Africa as long ago as June 26, 1955, reflect, more basically and simply, the aspirations of the African masses. The paragraph headed "The People Shall Share In The Country's Wealth" reads:

'The national wealth of our country, the heritage of all South Africans, shall be restored to the people.

'The mineral wealth beneath the soil, the banks and monopoly industry shall be transferred to the ownership of the people as a whole.

'All other industry and trade shall be controlled to assist the well-being of the people.

'All peoples shall have equal rights to trade where they choose, to manufacture, and to enter all trades, crafts and professions.

'Restrictions of land ownership on a racial basis shall be ended and all the land re-divided amongst those who work it, to banish famine and land hunger.

'The state shall help the peasants with implements, seed, tractors and dams to save the soil and assist the tillers.

'Freedom of movement shall be guaranteed to all who work on the land.

'All shall have the right to occupy land wherever they choose.

'People shall not be robbed of their cattle, and forced labour and farm prisons shall be abolished.'

The Freedom Charter was written as a reflection of South African conditions but all of it was applicable to one part of Africa or another, under colonial or racial rule.

Colonialism, the child of the industrial revolution, exported the beginnings of the industrial revolution to Africa. Colonialism, the child of the new capitalism in Britain and Europe, began the evolution which Africans with growing dedication are directing to the construction of socialism. Indeed, it is not too much to say that the most dynamic socialist movement in the world to-day is in Africa. It is the most comprehensively revolutionary continent. All of us, whatever our views, must recognise its significance.

2

Why Africa Turns to Socialism

How does it come about that so many of the African leaders are socialists? One reason is their age group. Most of them are between forty and fifty years old, which means that they were concluding their student days towards the end of the war, when socialism was at the top of a wave of popularity in Europe. British students came under the direct influence of the opinion which swept the Labour Party into power in 1945. At Oxford, Cambridge, London, Edinburgh, Manchester and other universities the undergraduates, particularly those who had returned from the forces, were in large numbers looking Leftward. The students from Africa eagerly responded to this mood. Perhaps even more important, their studies impressed upon them the close association between capitalism and imperialism, and its reflection in colonialism.

A considerable influence was the teaching of Harold Laski at the London School of Economics, attended by many Africans who subsequently became leaders. It is astonishing to find how many Africans now prominent sat at his feet, though the number of Indian statesmen who did so in pre-war years was even greater. Students at American universities came under similar influences. The Negro students at Lincoln University, American and African, responded excitedly to the sweeping advance of the Labour Party in Britain. President Nkrumah of Ghana and, earlier, Dr Azikiwe, now Governor-General of Nigeria, are examples. The formative thinking of Africa's political command was created at this time.

More recently, the lieutenants to Africa's political leaders have come under similar influences at the overseas universities; they have formed natural associations with Left students who have been most outspoken on the wrongs of colonialism. They have joined their own student societies, but they have also participated in the activities of organisations like the Movement for Colonial Freedom and the Africa Bureau in Britain or the Committee on African Affairs in America and felt at home in their Leftward and radical atmosphere. African students overseas now number tens of thousands; there are 18,000 from Commonwealth African countries in Britain alone. Many are taking advantage of invitations from communist countries. Efforts at indoctrination, wherever the students may be, often have the opposite effect to that intended. Young Africans have told me that students in Moscow tend to become anti-communist because they dislike the doctrinal rigidity of their studies, while students who come to Britain tend to become pro-communist because of their experience of colour feeling among our population. The total effect, whatever the location, has been to direct them towards some form of socialism.

There has been a clash in Africa between the European intellectual sources of socialism and the influences of Africa's social evolution. The result has been four trends in socialist theory, which can be summed up as Communism or Marxist-Leninism, African Marxism, African Pragmatic Socialism, and African Democratic Socialism.

The communists are active, but they have not acquired power in any influential African national movement or state. Marxist-Leninist ideology in Africa has arisen mostly from association with the French Communist Party and it is most evident in small groups of students and intellectuals in France's ex-colonies. They have scattered roots in Algeria in North Africa, in Senegal, Guinea, Mali and the Cameroons in West Africa, and in the Central African Republic. They have some influence in anti-government organisations of all races in

South Africa, and in every national movement enclaves of communists can be found. But, more especially after the struggle for independence has been won, the communists find themselves talking and striving against the tide of an Africanism assertively independent of any alien doctrine or commitment.

Two Marxist-Leninist movements have their headquarters in Senegal—the *Parti Africain de l'Indépendance* (*PAI*) and the *Fédération des Etudiants de l'Afrique Noire*. Their activities extend to surrounding territories, but they work under increasing difficulties because of the strengthening of one-party states. In the Central African Republic there is a Marxist-Leninist Youth Movement, the *Jeunesse Travailleuse Cubanguienne,* much repressed. In the Cameroons the *Union des Populations Camerounaises* was under strong communist influence and had considerable support while it was conducting guerrilla warfare against the French colonialist régime, but since independence and the assassination of its leader, Felix Moumié, in Switzerland, the support has waned.

In African trades unions communists are busy, but in this sphere, too, the trend is towards an Africanism independent of European influence. In the many one-party states of Africa communist parties are illegal; in some states, like the United Arab Republic, militant communists are imprisoned.

The Marxist-Leninists come into conflict with the general socialist flow in Africa because they insist that their 'scientific socialism' is authoritative under all conditions and that its theory and method must be universally accepted. The class struggle, the dictatorship of the proletariat and dialectical materialism must be totally swallowed. There is no such thing, in their view, as distinctive African socialism any more than European, Asian or American socialism. There is one socialism and *Das Kapital* is its infallible Bible. They argue, of course, that African socialists and socialist states should ally themselves with the Soviet Union, or (some of them) with communist China, but the leaders of Soviet Russia now appreciate that there is no early possibility of this. As a second best, they are prepared to accept African neutralism, uncommitted governments, independent national movements, independent trades unions, in the belief that at a later stage the struggle against imperialism, neo-colonialism and capitalism will bring them into the communist camp. Meanwhile, communist hold on Africa is surprisingly small.

The African Marxists are much stronger, Ghana, Guinea and Mali have governments whose leaders have all been strongly influenced by Marxism and, while they repudiate the rigidities of Marxist-Leninism and act at times vigorously against their own communists, they share with communist countries a monolithic state structure and authoritarian methods. One describes them as *African* Marxists because one of their complaints against the communists is that they are too servile to external pressures, whether from Russia or communist parties in Europe. Sékou Touré of Guinea once condemned the PAI as too French, too doctrinaire, and unable to make sufficient allowance for religious and community traditions peculiar to African peasant society.

In their pattern for the building of a socialist society the African Marxists differ from Marxist-Leninism in their flexibility, their neutralism, their willingness to accept aid from either the communist nations or nations of the Western bloc when it is provided without strings, their recognition that in the transition to socialism they are driven to accept priorities which involve sometimes the retention and even extension of privately-owned industries, their concessions on practical if reluctant grounds to American and European financial and capitalist interests, their tolerance towards the religious faith and practices of large sections of their populations, and their recognition that the traditional African social structure must not be destroyed but encouraged to evolve into socialism.

In contrast to the communist view that 'scientific socialism' is indivisible and imperative to all continents, African Marxists think and plan in terms of an all-African socialism, not merely modified to suit African conditions but original and creative in the experience of its own development. The African Marxists are largely responsible for the establishment of the African Federation of Trades Unions, which is independent both of the communist World Federation and of the Western-influenced International Confederation.

Thirdly, there are the African Pragmatic Socialists, dominant in the United Arab Republic and Tunisia in the north, in Senegal and Dahomey in the west, in Tanganyika in the east, and within many of the national movements in territories which have not yet attained full independence. They reject Marxism, the class struggle and the dictatorship of the proletariat. They are emphatically African, both Bantu and Arab, basing themselves on traditional social structures, accepted religions, and a culture which is subjective in contrast with dialectical materialism. They are ready to concede more to the private sector than the African Marxists, though they would subordinate it to a co-operative and collective economy.

Their governments are mostly based on one-party systems, characteristic of Africa, but generally, though not always, they allow wider political liberties than the African Marxist states. They are Pan-Africanists, but for the most part they put their faith in the emergence of African unity more by the development of common African economic services than by political integration.

African conditions—the labour pains which accompany the birth of nations—are not conducive to liberal societies, and democratic socialism, combining personal rights with economic collectivism, has only limited endorsement. But it was given a surprisingly challenging championship by the election manifesto broadcast by the Kenya African National Union (KANU) in April, 1963. This was the more commendable because of the disruptive circumstances in Kenya, the tensions of tribal loyalties, the presence of the European and Indian immigrant communities and the party divisions among Africans. KANU won the election and now has the difficult task of applying its enlightened philosophy in government.

In an introduction to the manifesto (produced with modern techniques of colour and pictures) Jomo Kenyatta states the principles of African democratic socialism in classical language:

'Our achievement of independence, for which we have struggled so long, will not be an end in itself. It will give us the opportunity to work unfettered for the creation of a Democratic African Socialist Kenya. *Democratic* because we believe that only in a free society can each individual develop his talents most fully to serve his fellow citizens. *African* because our nation must grow organically from what is indigenous; whilst adapting that which is suitable from other cultures from East and West, we must give our people pride and self-respect, building upon all that is good and valid in our traditional society. *Socialist* because political freedom and equality are not enough; our people have the right to be free from economic exploitation and social inequality.'

Except for its emphasis on democratic rights, the KANU declaration is similar to the political attitude of the Pragmatic Socialists. Kenyatta and his colleagues say that the Marxist theory of class war has no relevance to Kenyan conditions. They pronounce clearly for neutralism towards East and West, identifying themselves with all the peoples of Africa against Western imperialism but adding 'colonialism can take more subtle forms and can come from communist as well as from capitalist sources'.

They are no less Pan-Africanist than the Authoritarian Socialists, calling for a federation of independent African states not only for Kenya, Uganda, Tanganyika and Zanzibar, but opening the door to Nyasaland and the Rhodesias when they become democratically independent. An inspiring and constructive vision.

KANU does not foresee a restriction of trade union rights, but makes an appeal to the unions to realise their responsibilities to the rest of the nation, no doubt having in mind, as Nyerere and Senghor do in Tanganyika and Senegal, the prior claims of the peasants. The government will not as a rule nationalise the small sector of private industry because of the 'more urgent tasks for Kenya's scarce capital resources than buying out private owners', but it will take over industries or parts of industries when this proves necessary for the economy.

The government will itself initiate industries for the manufacture of finished articles from the agricultural produce of the country, but otherwise it will provide incentives to private investment since it will not have the available finance. It announces, however, that it will 'have no time for those who make large profits in Kenya and then fail to invest them in the country' and that it will exert a wide measure of control on the economy in the interests of the nation.

There is one passage which reflects that the libertarian aims of KANU embrace all human subjections. 'The inferior position allotted to women in most of our communities is contrary to the principles of social, economic and political democracy', the election manifesto insisted. 'It is an aspect of our country which attracts adverse criticism from visitors and one which shames us.' As one of those visitors I particularly welcome this affirmation. When, in 1950, I first raised this issue in Kenya, Jomo Kenyatta told me it was 'political dynamite'. Democratic socialists will earnestly hope that KANU will be able to live up to its ideals now that it is responsible for government.

* * *

Few of the African states reject the name socialist. The Ivory Coast government does so under the title 'state capitalism', but even it directs investment and participates in and controls a considerable sphere of industry. The French Congo and Liberia also repudiate socialism, the former because it is pro-France, the latter because it is pro-America. But surveying the broad scene, there is no doubt where Africa is moving.

European visitors to Africa, and still more particularly American visitors, are surprised by this eager acceptance of socialism. I remember a puzzled American professor exclaiming in Accra, 'My, these people take to socialism like ducks to water'. This is partly due, as we shall see in some detail, to the traditional pattern of African society, the tribes and the clans which owned so much in common and which were spiritually integrated as a community, a natural communism. This inbred kinship with socialism has been put well by de Graft Johnson, the widely-read young intellectual who is head of the Department of Sociology at the University of Ghana. He has described the affinity of the African historical community-pattern with socialism in this way:

'The principle of the State as a father, which is the basis of socialism, is what we have here in our clans or tribes which are in fact *extended families*. In our society, the collective wealth of the extended family is used for the welfare of the family as a whole. The extended families take on the functions of social insurance, and if a member of the family falls into debt, all the others help him to pay it; if he is ill, they look after him; if there is a bright boy in the family whom the immediate parents cannot afford to educate, the others help in educating him.

Property, especially land, often belongs to the whole extended family. There are abuses in the extended family system, but its basic pattern, when enlarged to embrace the state, is virtually what is meant by socialism.'*

The adaptation of the tribal system to complicated modern conditions presents, of course, enormous problems. It will mean, as all except the Marxist-Leninists realise, an African socialism different in many forms from either European social democracy or Soviet communism. To that subject we will return; but it is interesting to quote de Graft Johnson at once:

'What our social structure, which may be termed communalism, cannot cope with is the modern world with its capitalist industries, and our task here is to adapt the principles of socialism in industrial Europe to our own particular mode of life. Alternatively, we can develop our basic traditional institutions in keeping with the basic principles of communalism to fit modern conditions. I think we shall attempt both.'

Two African presidents, both belonging to the Pragmatic group, have written books on African socialism. The first is Julius Nyerere, president of Tanganyika, the second is Léopold Senghor, president of Senegal. They have risen to leadership from different political backgrounds but in many ways are strangely similar. Nyerere is the head of an African state on the east coast washed by the Indian Ocean; Senghor, of a state on the western bulge of Africa washed by the Atlantic. Tanganyika, a German colony before the First World War, has since been administered by the British, first under a mandate from the League of Nations, latterly as a trusteeship under the United Nations. Senegal has been under the very different colonial rule of France since 1904.

* *Drum*, September, 1962.

Both Nyerere and Senghor are Roman Catholics. They both come from the upper crust of African social life: Nyerere the son of a chief, Senghor of a prosperous family. They both went to European universities: Nyerere was the first Tanganyikan student at a British university, taking his arts degree at Edinburgh; Senghor was the first African to win an *agrégation* at Paris, qualifying him to teach in a *lycée* (high school). They both became socialists while at the university.

The similarity goes further. Neither Nyerere nor Senghor was ever racialist in an exclusive way. Nyerere was not anti-British. Senghor was not anti-French. When he became leader of the Tanganyika African National Union Nyerere spoke of the Europeans and Asians with such friendship that their elected members in the Legislature supported him as fully as the African members. When Senghor was taken prisoner during the war, instead of accepting a German invitation to lead an African rebellion against French colonialism he led a prisoner's mutiny against the Germans. He married a French wife, and when he formed a Socialist Party in Senegal he linked it with the French socialists. Yet both Nyerere and Senghor are deeply African.

The feature of Nyerere's inaugural speech as President of the Republic in the Tanganyikan Parliament in December, 1962, was his plea for pride in African culture. One must appreciate this fully if one is to understand how much African tradition and character—the African personality—are reflected in all their political thinking, not least in their socialism. This is a passage from the speech:

'I have set up an entirely new ministry: the Ministry of National Culture and Youth. I have done this because I believe that its culture is the essence and spirit of any nation. A country which lacks its own culture is no more than a collection of people without the spirit which makes them a nation. Of all the crimes of colonialism there is none worse than the attempt to make us believe we had no indigenous culture of our own: or that what we did have was worthless—something of which we should be ashamed instead of a source of pride. Some of us, particularly those of us who acquired a European type of education, set ourselves out to prove to our colonial rulers that we had become "civilised"; and by that we meant that we had abandoned everything connected with our own past and learnt to imitate only European ways. Our young men's ambition was not to become well-educated Africans, but to become Black Europeans. Indeed, at one time it was a compliment rather than an insult to call a man who imitated the Europeans a "Black European" .... So I have set up this new ministry to help us regain our pride in our own culture.'

Léopold Senghor is himself a poet and philosopher, admired as much in Paris as in Dakar for the music of his verses and the thoughtfulness of his writings. But he might have used exactly the same words as Nyerere. He has written this:

'Contrary to what many political Africans think, culture is not an appendix of politics which can be cut off without loss. It is not even a mere means to a political end. Culture is the beginning and end of all political philosophy worthy of the name.'*

It so happened that in December, 1962, I attended both a conference on African socialism in Senegal and the inauguration of the Republic of Tanganyika. I left Léopold Senghor to join Julius Nyerere. In both countries I heard the same tribute to their Presidents: appre-

* *Nation et Voie Africaine du Socialisme* (Présence Africaine, 42, Rue Descartes, Paris 5e). The author is indebted to Signora Ignazio Silone and Miss Joan Hymans for translations from this book.

ciation of their unassuming modesty and simple humanity. I have spent some time in trying to reflect them here because they represent the African personality as I know it best and because their socialism cannot be understood without understanding them.

The Swahili title of Julius Nyerere's book on the 'The Basis of African Socialism' is *'Ujumaa'**, which means 'Familyhood'. This word, he writes, 'describes our socialism'.

'It is opposed to Capitalism, which seeks to build a happy society on the basis of the exploitation of man by man; and it is equally opposed to doctrinaire socialism which seeks to build its happy society on a philosophy of inevitable conflict between man and man.'

Nyerere emphasises the basic idea, already quoted from the writings of the Ghanaian professor, de Graft Johnson, that socialism is a natural expanding development of the traditional tribal system of Africa. Every individual was completely secure in African traditional society. Natural catastrophe brought famine, but it brought famine to everybody. Nobody starved, either of food or of human dignity, because he lacked personal wealth; he could depend on the wealth possessed by the community of which he was a member. 'That was socialism. That *is* socialism.'

In traditional African society everybody was a worker. There was no other way of earning a living for the community. One of the most socialistic achievements of this system was not only the sense of security it gave to its members, but the universal hospitality on which they could rely. A Swahili proverb said, *'Mgeni siku mbili; siku ya tatu mpe jembe'*; in English, 'Treat your guest as a guest for two days; on the third day give him a hoe'. The basis of both security and hospitality was that every

* Tanganyika Standard Ltd., Dar-es-Salaam.

member of the community—barring only the children and the infirm—contributed his fair share of effort towards the production of its wealth. Not only was the capitalist or landed exploiter unknown to traditional African society, but neither did it have the loiterer or idler. Loitering was an unthinkable disgrace.

'The other use of the word "worker", in its specialised sense of "employee" as opposed to "employer", reflects a capitalist attitude of mind which was introduced into Africa with the coming of colonialism and is totally foreign to our way of thinking. In the old days the African had never aspired to the possession of personal wealth for the purpose of dominating any of his fellows. He had never had labourers or "factory hands" to do his work for him. But then came the foreign capitalists. They were wealthy. They were powerful. And the African naturally started wanting to be wealthy too. There is nothing wrong in our wanting to be wealthy; nor is it a bad thing for us to want to acquire the power which wealth brings with it. But it most certainly is wrong if we want the wealth and the power so that we can dominate somebody else.'

Nyerere acknowledges that some Africans have learned to covet wealth for that purpose, Africans who would like to use the methods which the capitalist uses in acquiring it.

'Our first step, therefore, must be to re-educate ourselves; to regain our former attitude of mind. In our traditional African society we were individuals within a community. We took care of the community and the community took care of us. We neither needed nor wished to exploit our fellow men.'

Recognition is given by Nyerere to the different backgrounds of European and African socialism and to the influence of these historical circumstances in the moulding of their distinct philosophies. European socialism was born of the agrarian revolution and the industrial revolution which followed it. The former created the 'landed' and the 'landless' classes in society; the latter produced the modern capitalist and the industrial proletariat. These two revolutions planted the seeds of conflict within society. Not only was European socialism born of that conflict; the conflict was sanctified into a philosophy. The class war was looked upon not as something evil, but as something necessary and good:

'As prayer is to Christianity or to Islam, so civil war (which they call "class war") is to the European version of socialism—a means inseparable from the end. Each becomes the basis of a whole way of life. The European socialist cannot think of his socialism without its father —capitalism!'

Nyerere adds that he finds this contradiction intolerable. It virtually says that without capitalism and the conflict which it creates within society there can be no socialism. But African socialism does not arise from the agrarian revolution or the industrial revolution. It does not start from the existence of conflicting 'classes' in society: it starts as a family society. Its objective is the 'extended family'. Africans have no more need to be 'converted' to socialism than they have to be 'taught' democracy. 'Both are rooted in the past which produced us.'

Nevertheless, Nyerere acknowledges that socialism must look to wider horizons for its 'extended family':

'Modern African socialism . . . can no longer confine the idea of the social family within the limits of the tribe, nor, indeed, of the nation. For no true African socialist can look at a line drawn on a map and say "the people on this side of that line are my brothers, but those who happen to live on the other side of it can have no claim on me"; every individual on this continent is his brother.

'It was in the struggle to break the grip of colonialism that we learned the need for unity. We came to recognise that the same socialist attitude of mind which, in the tribal days, gave to every individual the security that comes of belonging to a widely extended family must be preserved within the still wider society of the nation.

'But we should not stop there. Our recognition of the family to which we all belong must be extended yet further—beyond the tribe, the community, the nation, or even the continent—to embrace the whole society of mankind. That is the only logical conclusion for true socialism.'

Léopold Senghor's work, *Nation et Voie Africaine du Socialisme,* from which a quotation on the subject of African culture has already been given, is longer and more intricate that Nyerere's book. His philosophy and poetry make his writing both complex and subjective, but his contribution to socialist thinking is profound and deserves a recognition which it has not yet received beyond French-speaking Africa and France.

He is as firm as Nyerere in rejecting Marxism and European socialist theory. He, too, argues that Africa's social background of tribal community life not only makes socialism natural to Africa but excludes the validity of the theory of class struggle:

'Dictatorship of the proletariat? It is a formula for rattling in the throat! Must we have proletariat and capitalists at war before we can talk like Marx? In our Negro-Berber society . . . there is no class war, but merely social groups struggling for power to influence.'

The realities of West Africa—'underdeveloped countries, here peasants, there herdsmen, one-time feudal countries certainly, but traditionally without class or cash incomes, composed of communities where the group takes priority over the individual, religious, disinterested, where money is not king'—these, Senghor insists, make the analysis of European 'scientific socialism' irrelevant.

'It is, therefore, to betray Marx [he writes] to superimpose his method on to Negro-African, West African, realities. Above all, it is to betray him to superimpose on these realities, without attempting integration, the political, economic, social and cultural organisation of Europe, whether in its Western or its Eastern form: liberal Parliamentarianism or "peoples' democracy". It is paradoxically to betray not only Man but Negro-African—and by this I mean Negro-Berber—Humanism.'

Senghor rejects 'Marx's man in Africa', the European under a black or brown skin, the European beneath the Negro or the Berber. He rejects, like Nyerere, the 'class struggle for the conquest of buying power in a commercial world' as the ideal of civilisation.

He adds a still deeper reason for rejecting Marxism: something which he believes is inseparable from African psychology. He argues that the African approach to socialism is determined not only by the experience of traditional community living, but by the *'faculty of knowing'* which Africans have inherited. This is the supreme reason for 'not accepting blindly and without preliminary investigation' the materialistic European theory of 'scientific socialism', particularly dialectical materialism. His claim is put in these remarkable passages:

'We have inherited from our ancestors our own faculty of knowing. Why, then, should we change it just when the Europeans are telling us that it is precisely the twentieth century faculty and the most mature?

'Let us, therefore, consider the attitude of the Negro-African towards the Object to be known, towards the Other: God, Man, animal, tree or pebble, natural fact or social fact. Contrary to the classical European, the Negro-African makes no distinction between himself and the Object; he does not hold it away from himself to be examined or analysed; or rather, after having examined it, if not actually analysed it, he takes it in his hands, alive as it is, careful not to kill it and pin it down like a specimen. He touches it, he feels it, he is *conscious* of it. The Negro-African is like one of those verses of the Third Day, a field of pure sensation.

'It is by his subjectivity, with the tips of his sensory organs, with his insect's antennae, that he discovers the Other. We see him *ex-cited,* moving centrifugally from subject to object on the waves of the Other. This is more than a simple metaphor; contemporary physics have discovered, beneath matter, universal energy; waves and radiations.

'Here we have the Negro-African *sym-pathising,* leaving his ego to identify himself with the Other, dying to himself to be born again in the Other. He does not absorb, he is absorbed. He lives a common life with the Other; he lives in symbiosis, he has *cog-nition* of the Other, to use Paul Claudel's expression. Subject and object are here compared dialectically in the very act of *cog-nition.* Here is the long caress in the night, the locked embrace of bodies in union, the act of love.

'"I want you to be conscious of me", says an elector who wants you to know him well. "I think; therefore I am", wrote Descartes. But the remark no longer seems to have validity; one is always thinking; and the "therefore", a logician's conjunction, is meaningless. The Negro-African could say: "I sense the Other; I dance the Other; I am". Now, to dance is to discover and to recreate, particularly if the dance is a dance of love. It is in any case the best means of knowing. So that *cog-nition* is at the same time discovery and creation, or rather *re-*creation, and re-creation is the image of God.'

One cannot refrain from asking how far is this the philosophy and the poetry of Senghor rather than an image of Africa? Perhaps the truth is that it is the image of unsophisticated man, man with simple emotions and thoughts, intuitions unsuppressed. And so it is, in fact, largely African. Is it, as Senghor suggests, twentieth-century too? Does the modern scientific view that matter is composed of minutiae of energy emitting radiation endorse the intuition of ages of men whose only university has been Nature?

Senghor has a strong historical sense and from it emerges a creative sense, as this passage illustrates:

'Seen in its past context, colonisation would seem to be a necessary evil—having an historic necessity—from which good must come: on condition that we, yesterday's victims of colonisation, are conscious of the outcome and that we desire it. Slavery, feudalism, capitalism, colonialism, these are history's successive acts of parturition and, like all such acts, painful. With this difference, that in these cases the pains are suffered by the child more than by the mother. No matter! If we are fully conscious of the meaning of each new accession we shall cease to recriminate: we shall pay more attention to the contributions than to the failures, to the possibilities of *rebirth* rather than to death and destruction.'

We have seen that Senghor's analysis of the historical basis of African socialism is the same as Nyerere's. Nyerere would probably accept as African his 'faculty of knowing' in contrast with the method of dialectical materialism. But in his approach to political problems Senghor often differs from Nyerere and other African leaders.

He is cautious about Pan-Africanism, although fifteen years ago he moved a resolution at the Consultative Assembly of the Council of Europe in favour of a 'United States of Africa'. He leans to the West rather than towards neutralism. He rejoices that Senegal has retained its solidarity with France. In these respects he is closer to the ex-French colonies which have not followed him in his socialism than to the main stream of nationalist and socialist conviction in Africa.

But there should be no doubt about his socialism. The African contribution to socialism is a passion with him. 'Our realities', he says, 'are not the same [as those of Europe]. To remain faithful to socialism is for us—confronted with the new realities—to choose new methods, techniques and systems, the most modern, the most highly perfected. In a word, West Africa . . . must become one vast research laboratory. Nothing else matters but to give the world a model of a new country, creating a new civilisation in tune with the Africa and the world of the twentieth century.' As one reads these words one passes from Senghor, the poet and philosopher, to Senghor the realist, the planner. If he succeeds in this purpose he will certainly have contributed to Africa and the world.

3
The Socialist Sector of Africa

THE peoples of the greater part of Africa now have the political right to decide their own destinies. There are thirty-two independent African states* (excluding the Republic of South Africa) and within a few months Kenya, Nyasaland and Northern Rhodesia will join them. Where are they heading? How far are they committed to socialism?

It has been generally assumed that the ex-French colonies in West and Equatorial Africa were the least radical of the newly independent states. All of them, except Guinea, voted by referendum to stay within the French Community when in 1961 President de Gaulle offered continued association with France or independence. A year later they were recognised as independent, but the links with France, both political and economic, remained close. All but Mali and Guinea belonged to the Monrovia group of African states as opposed to the Casablanca group led by socialist Ghana and the UAR.

I was a little surprised, therefore, to receive an invitation to attend a conference in ex-French West Africa in December, 1962, on 'African Roads to Socialism'. It is true it came from Léopold Senghor, the socialist President of Senegal, but the list of the twenty-one Governments

* Algeria, Burundi, Cameroons, Central African Republic, Chad, Congo (Brazzaville), Congo (Leopoldville), Dahomey, Egypt (UAR), Ethiopia, Gabon, Ghana, Guinea, Ivory Coast, Libya, Liberia, Madagascar, Mali, Mauritania, Morocco, Niger, Nigeria, Rwanda, Senegal, Sierra Leone, Somalia, Sudan, Tanganyika, Togo, Tunisia, Uganda, Upper Volta.

who had agreed to participate* included many of the more conservative states which had emerged cautiously from the old French Empire.

I was also a little surprised, but delighted, to find that the conference bridged the gap between the Monrovia and Casablanca groups. Among the Casablancans, Algeria, Morocco, Guinea and Mali were in the list. Absentees were the UAR and Ghana. Kwame Nkrumah, I was told, had urged that the conference should be held in Accra. Nigeria, the largest of the African states, consistently active in striving to reconcile the Monrovia and Casablanca groups, was represented.

When I reached Dakar I found that not all the governments were committed to socialism. The subject of the conference had been modified to 'African Economic Development and Roads to Socialism' and some attended under the first item rather than the second. The Prime Minister of Niger, for example, made a speech urging that Africa must aim to combine 'the best in capitalism and the best in socialism'. But the tone of the conference was overwhelmingly socialist.

Léopold Senghor opened with an unqualified plea for socialism, and hesitant voices were few. This was very significant. It was clear that even in the areas of Africa which have been regarded as politically backward the dynamic trend is towards socialism.

Senegal

Senegal itself has gone far in the construction of a socialist society. It has co-operativised the whole of its agriculture, is establishing publicly-owned industries in

* Algeria, Cameroons, Central African Republic, Chad, Congo (Brazzaville), Congo (Leopoldville), Dahomey, Ethiopia, Gabon, Guinea, Madagascar, Mali, Mauritania, Morocco, Niger, Nigeria, Senegal, Sierra Leone, Somalia, Tanganyika, Tunisia.

village communities, and through the National Development Bank the government is acquiring 51 per cent of the shares in private industries when they are held by the bank to be financially sound.

Great emphasis is placed on village industrial development. Employment in the rural areas is seasonal; many workers are idle for nine months in the year and they flock into Dakar and other towns, existing in tumbledown shacks, still mostly unemployed, scrounging an existence. The object of the government plan is to provide work in village factories related to the neighbouring agricultural production. These factories are state-initiated and are run jointly with the agricultural co-operative movements and the Village Councils.

While in Dakar I learned that the then Prime Minister, M. Mamadou Dia, was pressing for a more radical advance to socialism. He had been to Russia and returned dissatisfied with a majority share of private industry. He advocated that it should be co-operativised as agriculture had been. Senghor advised caution, partly because he gave priority to the establishment of the publicly-owned village industries, partly because he did not want to scare away foreign capital which he held Senegal could not yet do without, and partly because he was aware that there were not enough trained African technicians to take over the duties which many of the French managements could be expected to desert. It was stated that agreement had been reached between President and Prime Minister but this was evidently not so. A few days later the Press reported that M. Dia had been dismissed by the President after an extraordinary incident in Parliament.

When the Prime Minister found that a majority of the Deputies were likely to carry a motion condemning him for suppressing liberties, he called in the police to evict them. The police obeyed, but in turn the army obeyed orders from the President to evict the police, and the public clearly demonstrated their support. The Prime Minister had apparently been influenced not only towards radical socialism but towards authoritarianism by the example of some communist régimes.

There was one tendency towards division in Senegal, which I subsequently found also in Tanganyika, related closely to socialist theory and practice. Senghor was emphatic in his warning to trade unionists, mostly urban workers, not to press their claims for higher wages to a level which would mean that they would have an undue portion of the national income compared with the peasants and agricultural workers, the more numerous of the wealth-producers of the country. Both Senghor in Senegal and Nyerere in Tanganyika used similar language. Senghor first paid tribute to Negro-African trades unionism which had played an essential part in the liberation of Africa and had produced some of its best political brains. He then went on:

'In spite of its past service, perhaps because of those services, trades unionism must now reconstitute itself, working out for itself a more precise idea of its proper place in our society and of its tasks.... The wage-earners, as the most educated social group and hence the most socially conscious, must look beyond, with strictly professional concern, their own sectional interests. By standing above the level of their own group, they can espouse the interests of all the social groups, and primarily of the most deprived, the peasants, herdsmen, fishermen, labourers....

'In Black Africa, civil servants and white collar workers, even manual workers, are bourgeois by comparison with the peasants, herdsmen, fishermen and labourers. It is a swindle to call the former the proletariat.... Salaries will not be lowered, but they will be blocked.... This will make it possible to use the savings realised for productive investment in agriculture, building, fisheries, crafts.'

Nyerere put the same point like this:

'It is one of the purposes of Trades Unions to ensure for the workers a fair share of the profits of their labour. But a "fair" share must be fair in relation to the whole society. If it is greater than the country can afford without having to penalise some other section of society, then it is *not* a fair share. Trade Union leaders and their followers, as long as they are true socialists, will not need to be coerced by the government into keeping their demands within the limits imposed by the needs of society as a whole. Only if there are potential capitalists among them will the socialist Government have to step in and prevent them from putting their capitalist ideas into practice.' Nyerere had previously argued that anyone in society seeking personal aggrandisement at the expense of the community is mentally a "capitalist".

At first sight the argument against excessive demands by trade unionists reads very much like arguments used in Britain for a 'wage freeze'. The difference is, of course, that Britain has mainly a free-enterprise economy based on personal gain, with disproportionate salaries for directors and managements and with extensive unearned incomes. Trade unionists can with reason argue that it is not 'unfair' for them as producers to demand a greater share of the national income while these disparities exist. These economic privileges do not, or should not, persist in a socialist society.

There is another important feature of socialist theory involved. Marxism has insisted that the urban proletariat would be the vanguard of the revolution and that the trade union struggle, beginning with wage demands, would be the means of the class struggle within capitalism and the precursor of the revolution. African socialism, in the context of an agricultural economy, clearly rejects this view. From the first, under socialist governments, emphasis is placed on the peasants and farm and plantation workers.

There are potential conflicts here. African trade unionism is militant, co-ordinated for the greatest part in an all-African Federation. It may not accept too readily the limitations of a controlled distribution of the national income. Indeed, we have already seen in Ghana strikes against savings deduction imposed in the interests of the national economy. We shall have to await events to see if the influence of the Nyereres and Senghors and their idealistic approach win the co-operative acceptance of the urban workers.

Dahomey

One of the most impressive speeches at the Dakar conference, impressive by its precise recitation of facts, was contributed by the Minister of Commerce in Dahomey, an oblong strip of territory lying between Nigeria and Togoland. I had not appreciated that independent Dahomey, another ex-French colony, has, equally with Senegal, deliberately set its compass towards socialism though I was aware of its bold and successful action in demanding Portugal's evacuation of its enclave at the Fort of John the Baptist in 1960: Portugal's first retreat on the African continent.

I once touched down in Dahomey while travelling by air from Accra to Khartoum. My memory is of neat palm tree plantations; its chief products are palm kernels and palm oil. The Minister described in detail how agriculture had been co-operativised and collectivised, and the next stage of socialisation planned is to establish publicly-owned industries associated with agriculture. It was very much the same pattern as in Senegal, except for the absence of majority shares in previously private industry. Industry hardly exists in Dahomey.

Mali

Two of the ex-French colonies which sponsored the Dakar conference are militantly socialist: Mali and Guinea. From 1958 to 1960 Mali was federated with Senegal; the federation was actually dissolved because Mali, its leaders indoctrinated by Marxism, wanted a more uncompromising socialism than Senegal was prepared to accept.

French colonialism in Mali had been particularly oppressive, and the new independent government in 1960 called for a complete break, the taking over of all the public services and the Africanisation of the civil service as well as the expulsion of the French armed forces. This was more than Senegal could assimilate at her then stage of development. She was becoming industrialised and required French capital and French technicians. When, on top of this, Mali and Senegal quarrelled as to who should be President of the Federation, it collapsed.

The Mali leaders started their socialist construction under great difficulties. The French had treated Mali as a Cinderella from whom little profit could be made. It was an area of desert and unfenced shrub land, without mineral resources. The French left it after seventy years without industries and only a fragment of transport. The per capita annual income was £17 compared with an average of £66 for the countries generally scheduled as underdeveloped.

President Modibo Keita outlined the ways and means of achieving a planned socialist economy at an extraordinary congress of the Sudanese Union (the governing Socialist Party) in September, 1960—'not slogans or ready-made formulas, but based on conditions in Mali linked with experience elsewhere'.

The plan for the 'Socialist Organisation of the Rural Society' has already begun operation. The African pattern of co-operativisation is followed. The officering of the co-operatives and the education of the membership are being carried out by teams drawn from the public services, the party, trades unions, and youth and women's organisations. In each village there are Rural Production and Mutual Aid Groups. This all-in voluntary service is, as we shall see, typical of Africa.

Particularly interesting is the method of education. Seasonal schools, with courses of twenty-five lectures on new agricultural methods, are held in district centres attended by young peasants. On completing the course each peasant is presented with a pair of oxen, a cart and a plough, advanced through a credit scheme. These young peasants become the moving spirits of their villages when they return.

An overall aim is to diversify the economy in contrast with the traditional colonialist policy based on the export of primary products to France at low prices. For this, transport is essential. A huge road programme has been begun; a more distant project is to build seven airfields; river navigation is being extended on the Niger. Power is equally essential. Dams are to be constructed at Sotuba and Sankarani. The industrial projects under public ownership are many, but they are worth listing to show their variety and their association with the basic agriculture. They include oilworks (ground nuts), sugar mills, ginneries (cotton), slaughterhouses and tanneries, cement works, salt mines, textile mills, flour mills, furniture and canoe-making, agricultural equipment (even motor-cycles and tractors), soaps, cigarettes, paper and bricks, and the tinning of fruit juices, vegetables and tomato purée. This is an indication of how a satisfying economy can be built on territory which has been regarded as primitive.

Mali's elaborate plan is being financed partly by loans from Russia and Czechoslovakia, but the intention is to meet the cost principally by internal effort divided into 'human labour' and 'monetary accumulation'. A Civic Service has been established and help is expected from everyone. (More about this later.) Three sources of internal finance are to be used: taxation, bank margins and profits from the public sector. Taxation revenue will be doubled. The revenue from the national bank and public sector profits must await the expansion of the economy.

Privately-owned industry is not excluded, but it will be admitted only if it conforms with the state plan, accepts profits fixed by the government and terms of later transference to public hands, admits government control of selling prices and managerial policy, and provides technical education for African personnel. It is too early to say how far private industrialists will be ready to agree to these drastic conditions.

Neglected Mali has a desperate task in the fields of education and health. Since the Sudanese Union came into power in 1957 there has been a devoted effort to train teachers and open schools; but, even so, only 10 per cent of the children of school age have been allotted places. At least 98 per cent of the population are illiterate. The enthusiasm for education is moving. Schools which will provide for 1,000 classes are being built by the Civic Service and voluntary labour. Plans include a Teachers' Training College, a secondary school with 900 boarders, a girls' grammar school, and a number of technical schools. A great drive against adult illiteracy has been begun through a network of Literacy Committees in the villages. One of the greatest crimes of French colonialism was its indifference to education in forgotten Mali. The same is true of the restricted provision for health. In 1959 there were only 174 dispensaries in the whole of Mali, each serving 23,000 people. The plans prepared by the Ministry of Health are detailed and thorough—the training of nurses and midwives, mass preventive medicine, sanitary education of the people, maternity and child welfare clinics, hospitals—but one reads them with some doubt. Only heroic effort will realise them. The work has begun heroically.

The leaders and people of Mali might well falter before their formidable difficulties. They are not doing so. As in other African countries, the construction of their new society has become a popular passion. It is led by the Civic Service, manned mostly by youth, who mobilise every able-bodied man and woman in the villages, even the elder children, into voluntary service, clearing sites, building schools, clinics, factories, roads, fences, dams, transporting equipment, furniture, machines. Particularly during the 'dead seasons' in agriculture, thousands of singing men and women march out of the villages to the nearest construction sites. We are witnessing a whole nation in rebirth. A question mark remains. Are Mali leaders too mechanically wedded to Marxist theory?

Guinea

Guinea was the only ex-French colony to vote for independence rather than autonomy within the French Community in de Gaulle's referendum of September, 1958. It was led to this decision by perhaps the most dynamic of all Africa's leaders, Sékou Touré, physically vigorous, strong of will, anchored in wide study of socialist philosophy and practice.

Sékou Touré came from the people. He was born of Moslem peasant farmers, began his education at a village school, emerging to a technical college in the capital, Conakry, from which he was expelled for leading a strike against poor food. That did not deter him. He continued his education by correspondence.

His first and, indeed, enduring love was the trade union movement. At twenty-three he became secretary of the Postal Workers' Union (he had a job in the telecommunications department) and in that capacity made his first contact with leaders abroad at the congress of the CGT (the strong French trade union federation, communist-led) in Paris in 1946. Two years later he was secretary of the CGT in Guinea and by 1950 of the CGT Co-ordinating Committee for French West Africa.

From the first Touré had an idealism beyond the material aims of the working-class struggle. In an interview quoted by Ronald Segal in his *African Profiles** he said: 'Trade unionism is a faith, a calling, an engagement to transform fundamentally any given economic and social régime, always in the search for the best and the beautiful and the just.' Like Senghor and Nyerere he soon came to reject the Marxist doctrine of the class struggle as irrelevant in the stage of history through which Africa was passing.

It has often been assumed that Touré is a communist. In fact he is the classical Africanist, unwilling to be the tool of any external Power or bloc of Powers, rejecting alike Western capitalism, European social democracy and Soviet communism. It was on this issue that he broke from the CGT in 1956, declaring that African trade unionism could only be weak when divided among three European ideologies. He founded a General Union of Black Africa, independent of both the reformist International Confederation of Free Trades Unions and the communist World Federation of Trades Unions. It was the advance guard of the similarly independent all-African Trade Union Federation established in 1961.

One of the purposes of the Union of Black Africa was to fight colonialism. As early as 1946 Touré had added political activity to his trade union campaigning. He was a founder member of the *Rassemblement Démocratique Africain* (RDA) which co-ordinated nationalist action throughout French West Africa. In 1952 he became secretary of the Guinea section of the RDA, the *Parti Démocratique de Guinée,* and in 1956, when the *la Loi-cadre* gave autonomy to the French colonies, he led the party to triumph, himself becoming Vice-President, virtually the Prime Minister. He was then thirty-four.

* Penguin Books, 6*s*.

'We prefer poverty in freedom to riches in slavery,' said Touré during the de Gaulle 1958 referendum. Certainly Guinea had to undergo poverty. France replied to its declaration of independence by withdrawing 4,000 administrators and technicians, doctors as well as craftsmen. I heard then from Guinea that typewriters and chairs as well as all administrative documents were taken from the offices. I also heard from my teacher friend of the poverty. Not only was food scarce, but all the elementary amenities, water, lighting, sewerage, disappeared.

Guinea under Touré pulled through. Ghana, little able to spare funds, loaned £10 million, a preliminary to a declaration of union between the two countries (Mali later joined), a gesture in anticipation of the union of all West Africa. The Soviet Union made a loan and, after Touré had visited America and China, their governments negotiated a trade agreement and a loan respectively.

It was probably these Russian and Chinese loans which fathered the conviction that Touré was committed to the communists. An event in Guinea soon made even Western statesmen think again. He expelled the Soviet Ambassador, Danil Solod, because he intrigued with the communist-led Teachers' Union in 'action against the state'. Officials were charged with supplying information to the Eastern bloc. Five of the union leaders were sentenced to terms of imprisonment varying from five to ten years.

Guinea's socialism is probably fuller than in any African state. The French withdrawal of managements meant that Touré had to take over all transport and industry as a supplement to his co-operativisation of agriculture. He has used the American trade agreement to diversify industry and a loan from West Germany to provide water supplies and roads. When France reconsidered its boycott, he even granted one of its companies a licence to exploit bauxite, but he terminated the contract when the directors failed to fulfil the condition that the processing to aluminium must be completed in Guinea.

Touré insists that any private company must serve Guinea's socialist plan.

One of the most remarkable of Guinea's achievements under independence has been its expansion of education. Despite all obstacles it is claimed that Guinea now leads all Africa in the number of children and adults studying for every thousand inhabitants. Touré is far from reaching the end of the road, but his determination, courage and strength promise much, not only for Guinea but for all Africa.

Algeria

Algeria was another ex-French colony which sponsored the Dakar conference, though, because of one of its endemic crises, the representative had not arrived before I had to leave.

Algeria's break with France was more drastic than Guinea's—the culmination of an eight years' war—and it begins its avowed object of constructing socialism in even more difficult circumstances.

President Ben Bella has announced a four-part programme. The 500 industrial units abandoned by the French will be run by 'workers' committees'; farms and plantations abandoned by the French will be run as collectives; Arab peasant farms will be co-operativised; the government will cut out middlemen and sell citrus and olives directly abroad through marketing boards. Ben Bella's original intention was to take over the oil and gas installations in the Sahara, the proceeds of which were to be divided equally between the French companies and Algeria under the terms of the Evian Treaty, but he has not enough technicians to assume management and he has had to postpone the realisation of this aim. The Algerian Government is beginning the building of a socialist society not only from grass roots but in territory where most roots have been destroyed. In addition to the devastation of the war is the effect of the flight of nearly one million Europeans who ran the major part of the economy outside the peasant farms.

I was present at the Independence celebrations in Algiers in July, 1963. There was extraordinary evidence of the dedication of government and people to socialism. They have put the war behind them; their one thought is the construction of a new society. For four hours a procession passed with every banner devoted to a socialist purpose. In the great vineyards elected workers' councils are successfully taking over the management. The mass desertion of the French has meant socialism from *below*, spontaneous self-government within plantations, factories and shops, rather than state socialism. There is still some chaos, but it was amazing to see the progress made.

Morocco

Morocco also had a constitutional crisis during the Dakar conference and its representative was absent. The constitutional crisis arose from the decision that at long last an elected Parliament would be allowed, the first since the late Sultan led his people to independence eight years earlier.

One cannot say that the Government of Morocco is by any tests socialist. But there is an influential Opposition which *is* socialist: a combination of intellectuals, trade unionists and dedicated democrats. I was at their earlier conference in 1962 in Casablanca and was impressed by their spirit and efficiency. They did less well in the elections than expected—the population in the rural areas was loyal to the Sultan—but my anticipation is that within a few years, despite the arrest of its leaders in the repression of August, 1963, the National Congress of Political Forces, or some of its more influential officers, will hold considerable power.

Africa is always throwing up interesting points of strategy for socialists. The Casablanca conference did so.

Moroccan socialists have to face one difficult obstacle: both the ownership of the economy (except the peasant farms) and its technical management are French. What is the best course to secure ownership with Africanisation? Which should come first—public appropriation or Africanisation of the management and technical staff?

This is a problem, of course, not peculiar to Morocco. I remember discussing it with Kenneth Kaunda, now the most influential minister in the government of Northern Rhodesia and its inevitable leader. How would he take over the copper belt companies when the management and technical staff were almost entirely European and non-co-operative? He answered that he would first Africanise the staff and then nationalise.

The Moroccan socialists reached a different decision. They would not aim at replacing the French managements and staffs by Africans; they would aim at gaining their support. They declared that all the productive personnel in Morocco, white-collar workers, executives and professionals no less than manual workers and peasants, Europeans no less than Arabs, would benefit from socialism. The exploiters were the French financiers in Paris who owned the Moroccan industries and plantations and drew Morocco's wealth to themselves. They would therefore set out to win the support of the French personnel. When that was accomplished, a Moroccan government could nationalise the economy without fear of breakdown.

There was some opposition to this view from the trade unionists in the conference, arising from conflicts which they have had with the managements; and one doubts whether the policy will be easy in practice, however correct it may be in socialist theory. The difficulty in Morocco is not, of course, so great as in Northern Rhodesia. In Morocco the French residents are those who elected to stay in the country at the time of independence and who have become accustomed to an African political administration. In Northern Rhodesia, in transition, a considerable part of the European managements, technicians and skilled craftsmen in the copper belt mines are with some difficulty adjusting themselves to the inevitability of a democratic constitution which would place whites and blacks in equality as citizens.

Tunisia

Tunisia is shaped like a man's head, crown northward to the Mediterranean, profile eastward, chin lifted, nose thrust upward. A challenge. A challenge to Europe from Africa.

There is something symbolical in this. Tunisia, squeezed between Algeria and Libya, with only four million people, is not only challenging Europe; it is defying Nature. It has few physical resources and no dependable rainfall. Yet with courage, skill and thoroughness it is constructing a new society.

Tunisia appointed three Ministers to attend the Dakar conference on 'Roads to Socialism'. Its government is regarded as moderate, and its socialism is pragmatic rather than doctrinaire. But few African nations have gone further in socialist planning.

France left Tunisia, to use the words of Habib Bourguiba, the President, in 'economic chaos'. The battle against underdevelopment he describes as harder and more complex than the battle for independence. The social and economic plan which Tunisia is operating is remarkably comprehensive and detailed. The problem is to modernise agriculture and integrate it with a new diversified economy.

The people are mostly peasants. The French did little for them. I have a vivid memory of an incident during a visit to Tunisia in 1960. We were driving to the Algerian frontier to see the refugee camps. In the hilly country the slopes were well terraced to prevent soil erosion. I assumed the French had done it. 'Not they', said my guide. 'That's all been done since independence.'

The French settlers, who took possession of the best land, have largely departed, and the state has taken over ownership and management. State farms occupy no less than 40 per cent of the agricultural land. Among the peasants an elaborate system of co-operativisation is being constructed, with the unusual feature of separate co-operatives for agricultural expansion, servicing (seeds, fertilisers, fuel, fodder, tractors, anti-parasite treatment, and the sale of the farm produce), irrigation, processing, The different societies are co-ordinated in a national federation linked with the Foreign Office for external trade.

France left Tunisia with industries only for the processing of agricultural and mining produce (very limited) and for the making of consumer goods. Expansion and diversification are now planned, particularly in the neglected south. The state will supervise the key industries, will serve as a partner with private investors in new industries, and will direct investment to the most useful development.

Education, health and housing are prominent in planning. The number of school places has been doubled in the six years since independence and at the present rate of progress every child of six should have a place by 1966. Secondary school places, now 30,000, should be 140,000 by 1970. The first university is being built.

The most striking development in the health service has been the network of maternity and child welfare units, some of them mobile; they are having an almost revolutionary effect in the villages. For so small a country the housing programme is impressive. The state is building 130,000 homes; 24,000 are being built through Workers' Co-operatives with state loans at 2 per cent interest; and 30,000 are being built privately.

No African country inspires more confidence in its constructive reliability. Present plans are to be completed by 1970. By then the old French Protectorate will be unrecognisable.

Nigeria

Nigeria, ex-British, the largest state in Africa with a population of over 35,000,000, was represented at the Dakar conference by a member of one of the government parties, and he declared himself unreservedly for socialism, but it would be too much to describe Nigeria as committed to socialism. The government is a coalition of the Peoples' Congress of the conservative North (which contains 60 per cent of the population) and the National Convention of Nigerian Citizens of the progressive South. There is a northern Prime Minister, Sir Abubakar Balewa, who has proved himself an able and reconciling statesman of this unusual alliance, necessitated by the supreme need to keep the Federation united. The Governor-General is Dr Nnamdi Azikiwe, the father of Nigerian (if not African) nationalism. Dr Azikiwe is an avowed socialist.

The Coalition Government has a record of splendid achievement in educational and economic development and the gulf between North and South is being steadily bridged, but the feudalism of the rural North, as distinct from its more radical towns, means that any socialist plan for the whole of Nigeria is not yet a political prospect.

The South is divided into three regions: East, West and the new Middle West, constituted in August, 1963. The East is the stronghold of the National Convention. In the West, the Action Group Party has been powerful. It was regarded as less radical than the NCNC, but in recent years it has declared challengingly for socialism and even for Nigerian membership of the Ghana-Guinea-Mali union. Towards the end of 1962, however, the Party split, the two sections engaging in a physical conflict in the Regional Parliament, leading to the declaration of a state of emergency. Chief Awolowo, the Party leader, was arrested and charged with treasonable felony and conspiracy; a commission alleged he had been guilty of planning a 'financial empire', which would be hardly consistent with socialist principles.

The new region, the Middle West, is likely to be won by the National Convention. One can say that three of Nigeria's four regions are moving, if slowly, towards socialism.

Sudan

No one would say that the Sudan is democratically socialist, but on its territory is to be found one of the most impressive socialist achievements on the whole continent: the Gezira scheme. In a triangle, with Khartoum its apex and the White and Blue Niles its long sides, a million acres of arid land have been converted into earth as fertile as anywhere in Africa. The annual earnings of the peasants in 1938, before the scheme began, averaged £38 a year. Now they reach £500.

The Gezira scheme is a partnership between the government and the peasants. It was initiated when Britain was responsible for the Sudan's administration. Arthur Gaitskell, brother of the late Hugh Gaitskell, was its architect. The fertilisation of the land was made possible by damming the Nile and channelling its rich water across the arid spaces. The peasants are organised as a vast co-operative and the revenue is shared with the government. There has been an extraordinary revolution in their lives: brick homesteads instead of mud huts; village halls, schools, clinics. No less than £75,000 is spent annually from the revenue on education, health, social development and agricultural research.

This is an inspiring example of what can be done by community effort. The results have been so impressive that the government has decided to extend the scheme by another million acres.

Tanganyika

From the Dakar conference on 'Roads to Socialism' I went to Dar-es-Salaam in Tanganyika for its republic celebrations. I have quoted at some length Julius Nyerere's views about African socialism. How does he plan to apply them in Tanganyika?

First, let there be no doubt about his socialist intention and spirit. His inaugural speech to the Council, as President, was unique outside communist countries in its avowal of socialist purpose. The sincerity of his socialist spirit was revealed when he amused a 10,000 African audience by describing the luxurious bed in which he had slept for the first time the night before in what had been the British Governor-General's palace, and the earnestness with which he begged the people to make their demands upon him so that he would not rest until every one of them had a comfortable bed.

Tanganyika began with the advantage of possessing one of the best organised co-operative movements in Africa, covering both coffee and cotton production. The coffee co-operative, on the slopes of Kilimanjaro, the highest mountain in Africa, has become almost a myth or an idol. It is not only economically successful; it has a college of education, a cultural club, a students' hostel. In fact, however, a rival co-operative is even larger, covering cotton production as well as coffee. The success of co-operation is authoritatively recognised. 'The co-operative movement has become well and widely established', remarked *Round Table* in its issue of October, 1962. 'It is understood and liked by the majority of African producers, and has not only brought with it great benefits to them but has become a predominant factor in the economic life of tens of thousands of Africans.'

Sisal, the main agricultural product in Tanganyika, is, however, still European-managed. By road north of Dar-es-Salaam, and still more by 'plane flying along the coast, one sees the neat plantations. The long-term policy of the Tanganyika government will be to co-operativise or collectivise these plantations, but at present it has too much on its hands and is without the necessary compensation finance to proceed. It has been satisfied with establishing a minimum wage for the workers.

In other directions, co-operation is being actively extended. Paul Bomani, the Minister of Finance, and others of his colleagues have been to Israel and are planning to adopt its methods. A Co-operative Bank has been established to serve the interests not only of the producer societies but to encourage savings by workers generally. A Consumer Co-operative Organisation has been set up, Israeli-managed and partly Israeli-financed. At present wholesale trade is largely in European hands and retail trade is almost entirely Asian. The object of the Consumers' Co-operative is to encourage urban Africans to participate and to give them a shared benefit of the proceeds.

The government's first purpose, however, is with the peasant farmers. Outside the co-operatives and plantations, they are scattered in isolated huts over the bush country, with small unfenced plots of banana trees and coffee and sisal plants about them. Their agriculture is primitive, they are without near-by water, they have to go long distances for shopping, the children have little opportunity to get to school. The government is keen to develop a new village structure, where water and electricity supplies, education facilities, shopping centres, dispensaries and medical clinics, a village hall and, in time, a factory associated with their produce are available. It was good to see outside Dar-es-Salaam an old prison converted into the Village Development Research Department headquarters.

Nyerere and his colleagues are giving first priority to this task. During the next three years £23 million are to be expended on the modernisation of agriculture, water supplies, electrification, roads and irrigation. The cost will be met by grants and aid from Britain totalling £7 million, external loans of £11 million, internal loans of £4 million and £1 million from local revenue.

Plans for the socialisation of industry are still modest. The diamond industry at present is 51 per cent government-owned and this may be extended. Plans are being considered to nationalise the stevedoring companies with a view to the allocation of profits to the dockers' union and the national revenue. Nyerere's concern that the trade unions, mostly composed of urban workers though extending to the plantations, should not gain wage increases at the expense of the rural population has already been recorded. There may be conflict here. On the initiative of the government, Parliament has passed a law making strikes illegal and imposing considerable governmental control of the unions in return for their participation in industrial management. In justification, it is urged that in a community planning for socialism the trades unions should not take sectional action and that their function is to co-operate constructively with the administration. Time will show whether the trades unions will accept these limitations. Tanganyika's Vice-President, Mr Kawawa, as well as Mr Kamaliza, the Minister of Labour, was a former President of the Federation of Labour. They should know the minds of the unions.

One found in Tanganyika a repetition of the inspiring story in other African states of the enthusiastic co-operation of the people in construction. Here, too, men, women and teenagers were proudly building roads, schools, clinics, village halls, irrigation channels in the evening hours and at the week-ends. It was infectious to hear them singing and laughing as they worked. These voluntary working parties demonstrated, even more than the cheering, dancing, crowds in Dar-es-Salaam, green branches like a wind-swept forest above their heads, the determination of the people to make something good of their Republic.

Uganda

A little earlier my wife and I had been invited to the independence celebrations of Uganda. One cannot call its government socialist. The Prime Minister, Mr Obote, is a socialist and his United People's Party is typical of African Left nationalism, but his government is a coalition with the Kabaka monarchists from Buganda and must move slowly. There is, however, a curious contradiction among the Kabaka's followers. They are loyal to him and his royal status, but when I had lunch with a group of his ministers I found them no less progressive, no less socialistic, neutralist and Pan-African, than UPC members of the Government. The two loyalties will probably be resolved by the Kabaka becoming the constitutional Governor-General or President of the whole of Uganda.

Uganda has a good basis for the common African pattern in its co-operative movement. The greater part of its cotton production, its richest resource, is co-operativised. Indeed, it was the Farmers' Co-operative Union which led the struggle for independence thirteen years ago. Since then it has controlled not only the production of the raw cotton, but the processing plant of the ginneries.

Uganda started independence with the advantage of no white settler land-owning population. The treaties establishing the Protectorate laid down that no land should be alienated and only very limited exceptions have been made to this rule. There is comparatively little industrialisation except for a copper mine on the slopes of the Mountains of the Moon, privately leased but with provisions which require the training of Africans in skilled jobs.

I was interested to find that the excellent series of hotels are nationalised, though the managements resented a concession which had been given before independence to an Italian firm to start a chain of motels. My expectation is that Uganda will move towards socialism as certainly as other African states.

* * *

The socialist sector of Africa—the territories with independent governments which have a declared socialist purpose—now includes the United Arab Republic, Tunisia, Algeria, Mali, Senegal, Guinea, Ghana and Tanganyika. In addition, Uganda, as we have seen, and the Congo have socialist Prime Ministers, though the latter has frightening constitutional problems not limited to Katanga which will delay him in economic planning.

The socialist potential of Africa is, however, much greater than this sector. At an early stage we shall probably have socialist-pledged governments in Kenya, Zanzibar, Nyasaland and Northern Rhodesia. Among existing sovereign states, Somalia is likely to endorse socialism, the United Arab Republic may influence Sudan and Libya, and the triumph of the socialist Opposition in Morocco cannot be delayed beyond a few years. On the other hand, Nigeria will be held back for a time by its conservative North; in Sierra Leone the socialists are at present a small Opposition! Gambia will unite with socialist Senegal; Ethiopia will remain for a period as a paternalistic monarchy; Liberia is too closely linked with America to espouse socialism easily; and the ex-French colonies in West and Equatorial Africa which have not followed Senegal, Guinea and Mali are closely linked with Paris.

The southern area of Africa—Southern Rhodesia, the Portuguese territories of Angola and Mozambique, South West Africa and the Republic of South Africa itself—

has still to pass through a hard struggle before the democratic opportunity is gained for the peoples to decide their social pattern; but it is significant that their African leaders are almost without exception socialists. In the three British Protectorates—Bechuanaland, Basutoland and Swaziland—progress towards democracy is being made, and here too the leaders of the progressive African parties are mostly socialist.

As will be emphasised in our final chapter, the achievement of socialism in Africa—educated peoples consciously co-operating in economies which they own, lifting themselves from primitive conditions of tribal existence to the amenities of modern civilisation—is still a distant prospect, involving many years of creative effort in schools, technical colleges, universities, clinics, hospitals, administrative experience, economic planning, management and service. But the great change has begun. The makers of the New Africa have seen the vision, many of them are proving their capacity for the task, and they are enrolling a growing army of followers dedicated to the purpose.

Two nations in Africa have given leadership in their socialist planning—Ghana under President Nkrumah and the United Arab Republic under President Nasser. They have shown themselves to be the most challenging and controversial in the policies which they have pursued. Their stories, since President Nkrumah became head of the independent Ghana and President Nasser overthrew the monarchist order in Egypt, have been explosively exciting, involving criticism and dispute in most of the world. In Ghana and Egypt the problems and difficulties of fashioning socialist societies under African conditions can be seen in the most dramatic form. Their experience calls for detailed and fuller examination.

4
The Socialism of Nkrumah

GHANA is subject to much doubt and some denunciation. Many people in Britain and other politically democratic countries are concerned about her detentions without trial, her decision to become a one-party state, her deification of President Nkrumah and about the danger of dictatorship. Later in this book the implications of one-party states, centralised power and the limitation of liberty will be considered. But when criticisms of Ghana are voiced there is rarely any recognition of the historical and political circumstances which have led to its present course, nor of the remarkable social and economic transformation which has taken place since independence.

It is interesting that the Duke of Edinburgh, who often expresses welcomely independent views, was led to remark with sincere spontaneity during his stay in Ghana in 1959: 'If the only thing which this visit achieves is to draw outside attention to your inspired efforts to develop your country, I shall be more than satisfied. I would like all the world to know what you are doing.'

The decisive step which launched Ghana towards socialism occurred before self-government was attained. It took place within the nationalist movement. I was with Kwame Nkrumah on the evening when he received the invitation to become secretary of the United Gold Coast Convention. George Padmore, whose zeal for both Pan-Africanism and socialism influenced the future president greatly in his student days, was also there. Nkrumah hesitated before replying. Although he had obtained his degree in America, he had begun a course of studies at the London School of Economics, and he was doubtful about the United Gold Coast Convention: it was led by chiefs and the professional bourgeoisie and was not the popular mass movement which he knew was imperative to gain Ghana its freedom. Ultimately, urged by George Padmore, he decided to go and to devote himself to broadening the appeal of UGCC.

In Ghana he began plans to establish bases in the villages for the national movement, to create a youth movement and to bring in the market women in the towns. The leaders of the UGCC took alarm; fearing loss of power, they first obstructed his efforts, then forbade them. Nkrumah resigned and announced the formation of the Convention Peoples' Party, to be rooted in the masses. At first he had a lean time, often without food or bed as he travelled about the country. Then the people responded. He was soon hailed with enthusiasm everywhere he went. There was a demonstration of ex-servicemen in Accra which clashed with the police. Nkrumah and several of his colleagues were sentenced to imprisonment.

While he was still in prison, in 1951, the first general election took place. His CPP was swept to office, winning 34 of the 38 seats. The prison gates were opened for Nkrumah to become Leader of Government Business, soon to be designated Prime Minister. Ghana was not then independent, but it had considerable self-government. Within these limits Nkrumah began to apply the socialist principles which had led him to democratise the national movement.

I was in Ghana in 1956, a year before independence. I remember a high English civil servant saying that he had been asked to do more constructive work during the five years of Nkrumah's period of office than he had done in his previous twelve years of service in Ghana. I travelled to the far distant north, regarded as primitive. In an isolated village I saw a newly established, well-equipped dispensary, a small hospital with wards for men and women and an operating theatre; the notices were in pictures because the people could not read. I asked a woman drawing water from a tap at the village centre what she thought of Nkrumah. 'He is a good man', she said. 'He has brought us water. Before, we had to carry it three miles in petrol tins.'

It was only when Ghana gained independence in 1957 that Nkrumah could plan for socialism as fully as he desired. He summoned George Padmore from London; it was a disaster when Padmore died. But the plan survived and emerged. Nkrumah has been advancing its application ever since. In his Christmas Eve broadcast in 1957 he used these words:

'My first objective is to abolish from Ghana poverty, ignorance and disease. We shall measure our progress by the improvement in the health of our people; by the number of children in school and by the quality of their education; by the availability of water and electricity in our towns and villages; and by the happiness which our people take in being able to manage their own affairs. The welfare of our people is our chief pride, and it is by this that my Government will ask to be judged.'

I think what follows will show that the judgment on this test cannot be other than favourable.

President Nkrumah has said that a revolution is being carried out within Ghana, but in fact the plan of transformation recognises the limiting circumstances of considerable dependence upon foreign investment and technical assistance from abroad. There are two alternatives for the emerging nations of Africa. They can follow the Russian pattern of accumulating their own capital by imposing a period of privation on their peoples and by dictatorial regimentation, particularly of the landowning peasants; that brought great cruelties and tyranny in Russia. Or they can combine an invitation to foreign investors and technicians to participate in essential projects under conditions which will not rule out socialisation in the future, while at the same time demanding a certain sacrifice from their own people to finance general social and industrial development. The Ghana government has adopted the second method.

President Nkrumah's socialist plan has four parts:

1. The state-owned sector
2. Joint state and private enterprise
3. The co-operative movement
4. Private enterprise.

The state-owned sector includes electricity and water supplies, hydro-electric projects, arms and ammunition, and alcoholic beverages. These services and industries are administered by an Industrial Development Corporation on behalf of the nation. The Corporation also steps in when other desired production is not functioning under private enterprise. When I was last in Ghana it was running an efficient factory for making furniture from Ghanaian timber, a brick-making works and a modern printing establishment to produce daily newspapers, government documents and state-sponsored books. Generally speaking, however, the public sector in the Ghana plan (excluding agricultural co-operation) is not more extensive than in the mixed economy of Britain.

The second part of the plan, concerned with enterprises jointly owned by the state and private companies, is still largely a matter of intention rather than of fulfilment. The idea is to insist upon state participation in monopolies whose interests might become incompatible with public interests and in industries which require some state protection or assistance, as, for example, where protective tariffs are claimed or where private enterprise is not prepared to operate without government help. This proposal goes beyond the practice in Britain, where Conservative governments have refrained from claiming a share in ownership even when state subsidies are provided. A Labour government would probably accept the Ghanaian principle.

Like other African nations, Ghana gives far more prominence to the co-operative movement than do the economic plans of socialist parties in industrial countries with which we are familiar in Europe. Indeed, this is the most important basic structure in its present socialist planning.

The main productive activity in Ghana is cocoa. Before the Second World War the cocoa farmers were at the mercy of the middlemen who bought their crops to sell to the British and American cocoa and chocolate firms. The prices which they received were generally low. Moreover, they had no security. World prices fluctuated, and the farmers were often left without resources by an unforeseen drop in payments for their produce. They had to resort to money-lenders who were not infrequently unscrupulous and who exploited their ignorance and their needs. The smaller farmers suffered long periods of anxious poverty.

During the war the overseas market for Ghana's cocoa crop largely disappeared. Consumption was cut in the United Kingdom and shipping was reduced to a minimum. The British administration in Ghana, eager to retain the goodwill of the people in war time, was compelled to introduce certain controlled marketing arrangements to assist the farmers, including guaranteed prices for the stocks which were accumulating. The cocoa growers found, despite the fact that their product was unsaleable on the world market, that they enjoyed a security which they had not previously known.

This resulted in two decisive developments after the war. The first was the wide growth of a voluntary co-operative movement among cocoa farmers, who discovered that by pooling their product and selling it in bulk to the British and American exporters they could overcome the exploitation by the middlemen. The second advance was the establishment by the government in 1947 of the Cocoa Marketing Board, which again excluded the middlemen by buying direct from the farmers and at the same time provided security by guaranteeing prices for the crop year.

At first there was some conflict between the voluntary co-operatives and the Marketing Board on an issue of principle which afterwards caused some controversy over the whole sphere of co-operative activities in Ghana and led to a clash with the International Co-operative Alliance. The historic basis of the co-operative movement since the days of the Rochdale Pioneers has been the voluntary association of its members. It has resisted state intervention and compulsion. The first challenge to this came from Russia, but rather uneasily the Soviet co-operatives have been accepted as part of the International Alliance.

In Ghana the government has also aimed to integrate the co-operative movement with its national economic planning; thus, when rivalry occurred between the cocoa co-operative pool and the Cocoa Marketing Board in selling their supplies to the British and American exporters, the government imposed co-ordination.

Two systems had run side by side. The co-operative farmers sent their products to their own central agency; other farmers sent theirs to the Marketing Board. The solution was reached that the entire supplies should be taken by the Ghana Farmers Marketing Co-operatives and that there should be no other licensed agents to buy the cocoa from the individual farmers. This might be regarded as a co-operative victory, but it destroyed the voluntary principle of co-operation and involved partnership with the state in management. On the other hand, and perhaps more importantly, it undoubtedly gave the opportunity for efficient co-ordination.

Another issue has arisen. How far should the revenue from cocoa production be returned to the farmers and how far should it be allocated by the state? The farmers, particularly the co-operative farmers, argued that the revenue should be theirs. I had met the same problem in 1950 in Uganda, where the Cotton Farmers' Co-operative Union claimed that it should have the right to sell its produce at world prices and enjoy the full proceeds, rather than hand it over to the government Marketing Board, receiving only the payment which the Board determined after keeping a reserve in good years to meet contingencies in bad years—clearly a far-seeing device.

There was, however, this fundamental difference between Uganda and Ghana. The Uganda farmers then regarded the government, which was essentially colonialist, as the instrument of an alien occupation. They were rebels against it; their union had been declared illegal; they were not prepared to co-operate with it. In Ghana the colonial régime had been ended. The government was Ghanaian, the choice and voice of the people. The revenue from the cocoa farms was by far the largest source of national wealth. The government therefore insisted that it should contribute to Ghana's great plans for national construction and social development. This principle was made clear by President Nkrumah when opening Cocoa House, the magnificent headquarters of the Marketing Board, in November, 1960: 'The accumulated reserves of the Cocoa Marketing Board are public money, held in trust by the Government for the benefit of the farmers and the people of this country.' Most of the cocoa farmers patriotically accepted this, appreciating the security which it afforded them.

A large part of the reserve funds has been devoted to the development of the cocoa industry itself. For example, £27 million were contributed towards cocoa rehabilitation and control of the swollen root disease and other diseases, and an endowment of £2 million was given to the faculty of Agriculture of the University of Ghana. Another £2 million was donated to the West African

Cocoa Research Institute in aid of the study of cocoa disease and the cultivation of high-yielding varieties. But Ghana's cocoa wealth has also contributed to the advancement of the nation in health, education, social services and wider economic development. Regional organisations have received grants of approximately £3 million to finance local development projects; the construction of a hospital in memory of Tettah Quarshie, who first introduced cocoa into Ghana, has been financed, and money allocated for the construction of forty secondary schools.

In all, £74 million have been provided by the Marketing Board for the development and improvement of agriculture, health, education, economic development and social services.

An impressive illustration of how a government which has the goodwill of the people can overcome difficulties threatening an industry was given when Ghana's cocoa was menaced by the devastating swollen root disease. No successful treatment of the disease had been discovered and the only course was to cut down the affected trees to prevent infection spreading. The attitude of the farmers to this drastic remedy, when proposed by the British administration in 1951, repeated the reaction which I have described among the cotton farmers in Uganda to orders from their colonialist rulers. They refused to allow the government's officials on their farms, demanding that some alternative method of dealing with the disease be found, other than destruction of the trees.

In London I received angry cables calling for protests in Parliament and appealing for consultations with agricultural scientists. I met leading specialists and the Colonial Office experts, but to no avail. It became clear that no curative treatment was known. The opposition of the Ghana farmers persisted, however, and was so strong that the government had to abandon its plan for the compulsory cutting down of the trees. The disease spread.

Then Kwame Nkrumah became responsible for self-government in Ghana. Somehow he had to rescue the cocoa industry. He adopted a new approach, persuasion instead of compulsion. He arranged for members of the agricultural research staff to meet the farmers with trusted Africans. He offered generous compensation for loss of trees. Many farmers became convinced, and a voluntary cutting down scheme was started; only when a majority of farmers agreed was it made compulsory. By the end of 1960 all the cocoa-growing areas in Ghana had been surveyed, diseased trees had been rooted out, and regular inspection introduced. Ghana's cocoa industry was saved. A notable example, this, of how self-government, co-operation and persuasion are more effective than orders by a distant authority, especially an alien authority. The spirit of democracy triumphed.

By accident I became more closely involved in the development of another co-operative venture in Ghana which has become important. I have told elsewhere how seven years ago an African diamond winner (licensed to gather diamonds from designated land), a Welsh businessman and a City of London diamond merchant asked me to use my influence to enable them to establish a distributing agency for Ghanaian diamonds in London. I refused to have anything to do with it unless it were made part of a co-operative scheme. From that point the City merchants lost interest, but the Welshman, Mr Willis Griffiths by name, had a socialist background and he has since devoted himself with persistent zeal to the idea of encouraging the Africanisation of the diamond industry on co-operative lines.

Later I went to Accra with Mr Griffiths and together we submitted a scheme to President Nkrumah for the co-operative association of the diamond winners on lines similar to the cocoa-growers' organisation (in fact, some of the winners had already begun co-operatives), for the training of Africans to serve as valuers, polishers and graders of the diamonds, and for the setting up in London of an agency under African control for placing the diamonds on the world market. In other words, for the complete Africanisation of the industry so that its wealth should be enjoyed by Ghana.

The scheme met with violent opposition from the vested interests in the diamond industry and obstruction involved frustrating delays, but by 1962 plans had been endorsed by the government to place 40 per cent of the diamond industry of Ghana, from the winner on his land to valuation and processing, on a co-operative basis, and in 1963 a Marketing Board was set up to sell the Ghanaian supply to dealers. All that remained to be accepted was the establishment of an agency under Ghanaian control to market the diamonds directly.

The development of the diamond industry in Ghana has been fantastic. In 1950 the production was a little over 500,000 carats. By 1959 it had become 1·86 million carats, valued at £65·2 million. Ghanaian diamonds are mostly suited for industrial purposes, for which the world demand is great.

The expansion of the diamond industry is part of the Ghanaian plan to save the economy from dependence upon cocoa production. A one-industry state is always precarious: if prices fall, the whole economy is affected. Ghana's first socialist plan concentrated on the rehabilitation of the cocoa crop by saving it from the swollen root disease and encouraging the farmers by security as described above. It succeeded: in 1958 the cocoa crop had fallen to less than 200,000 tons; in 1959 it had risen to nearly 300,000 tons.

Ghana's second socialist plan, begun in 1959, placed emphasis on the diversification of agriculture. Bananas, coffee, coconuts, copra, kola nuts, rubber, tobacco were recognised as products which could supplement cocoa, as well as cattle-ranching on the grasslands.

This diversification was not only desirable to give balance to Ghana's economy; it was necessary to provide food for the growing number of workers in the towns. Indeed, demands arising from the higher standards of life of the extending urban population became a real problem. To meet them, food had at first to be imported from abroad. In seven years food imports had doubled, causing a strain on the balance of payments. Ghana had to grow more food for itself or run into financial difficulties. State concentration on this purpose triumphed. In fact, the new diversified crops not only went far towards meeting the needs of the urban workers; they contributed to meeting the balance of payments problem by exports. Exports of bananas rose from 19 cwt. in 1950, to 28,099 cwt. in 1959. Coffee production rose from 2,058 cwt. in 1950 to 39,644 cwt. in 1959. The output of tobacco has grown to more than two million pounds compared with 750,000. Appreciable increases have been recorded in coconut, copra, kola nuts and rubber.

These developments have taken place as the result of planned initiative by the government's agricultural department. It finances a Development Corporation which encourages the formation of farmers' co-operatives and takes full advantage of United Nations advisers. It is planning development according to natural conditions. Banana and rubber plantations are set up in the wet south-west; cattle-ranching in the grassy north, the south-eastern coastal savanna and the Accra plains; market gardening near Accra, Nsawan and in the Volta region. A stream of help is given in the use of fertilisers, seed dressings, new varieties, improved husbandry techniques, mechanised cultivation in suitable areas, the distribution of seedlings at cheap prices, credits for tools and equipment, and a service of tractors. Irrigation and soil and water conservation have been developed, including the construction of 113 dams in the northern and upper regions.

As a result of these activities, the prospects are encouraging. There are hopes, for example, that the rubber estate in the neighbourhood of Takoradi will in time provide the basis for an industry with an annual value as great as that now derived from cocoa. The larger plantations are state-owned but the general pattern is co-operative farming, with some instances of private enterprise, particularly in modern poultry farming. Broadly speaking, an African pattern of agricultural socialism is emerging, state-planned and serviced, co-operatively run, comprehensive, nation-wide. This is a noteworthy example of socialist construction on the African model.

Accompanying this revolution in agriculture has been a revolution in fishing. Ghanaian practice has been primitive, if picturesque. One has seen the long canoes flashing through a crescendo of waves. When in 1956 I met deputations of villagers in central and northern Ghana there were strong complaints that they did not benefit from the fishing on the coast. This was the record of advance which President Nkrumah gave at the State Opening of Parliament in July, 1961:

'Our fishing industry is undergoing a revolution: the motorisation of our traditional canoe fleet, the rapid growth in our fleet of motor fishing vessels, together with the establishment of cold storage plants in inland areas and of the cold stores plant and canning factory in Tema, will in a few years radically transform the diet of our people by providing them with adequate supplies of high quality protein, which we need so much.'

All this represents a record of construction of which any nation might be proud; but Ghana's two greatest endeavours, the Volta River project and Tema Harbour, have yet to be described.

The Volta River project is fantastic. It has been for more than ten years a dream of President Nkrumah, dismissed by many, sometimes with a cynical smile, as a dream unrealisable. It has met with rebuffs which would have broken the purpose of a less determined man: financial hopes dashed, withdrawals by industrial collaborators, a thousand constructional difficulties. But now the idea begins to be clothed. At Akosombo, destined to be the port on the largest man-made lake ever created, roads, houses, water pipe-lines, the nucleus of a modern township, are being constructed to welcome the engineers and the 3,000 workers who will complete the project.

The builders of the new Ghana realise that if it is to become wealthy, so that the standards of life of its people, their material conditions, health, education and cultural fulfilment, may become the equal of those of Europe and America, their agricultural advance must be accompanied by an equal industrial advance. The first need of industry is power, electrical power to drive machinery, to process materials, to facilitate refrigeration, to operate chemical processes, to smelt minerals. The Volta River project will provide that power over the major part of central and southern Ghana, the potential industrial sector, to Tema, the great new port on the coast, through Accra to Takoradi along the coast, to Tarkwa, Dunkwa, Kumasi, the capital of the Ashanti, on to Koforida and back to Akosombo. Not only will modernised factories, workshops, warehouses and mines be possible, but modern cities, lighted streets, electricity in the houses of the people. The face of Ghana could be transformed.

The Volta river varies in flow in the ratio of as much as 300 to 1 between flood and low water. The flood now runs to waste. The project will store the water in a vast lake covering 3,275 square miles, providing a reserve for the low water season, enabling a constant flow through the great dam which will generate the power. The dam will be 370 feet high and 2,100 feet in width. The power house will take six generators, each of 128,000 kilowatts continuous output. It is claimed that when completed the lake, the dam and the power station will be one of the major engineering feats of the world.

Even here the President's unfolding dream does not end. The lake will provide a new highway to the distant north, helping to break down its isolation and backwardness; but not only that. American engineers are now conducting a survey on the prospects of continuing the water highway to the sea, so that ships may transport materials from the coast to the furthest region of Ghana and bring back cattle and agricultural produce to the towns of the south and to be transmitted overseas.

There are more immediate advantages. The lake will create a new fishing industry: it is estimated that eventually 10,000 tons of fish a year will be available. And the six hundred square miles of land around the shores of the lake will be flooded each season at high water, amenable to intensive cultivation of crops such as rice. The project will provide large new sources of food no less than of power.

There is an incidental feature of the project which promises to be unusually pleasing, apart from its material purposes. Speaking of the new township at Akosombo, President Nkrumah says: 'One of the criteria which has been adopted is that of keeping the site of the dam and power station free from ugly and depressing buildings, so that the area can be made into a true attraction for tourists, not only because of the worldwide interest which so great a project will arouse, but also because the area will be made into a delight to the eye.' One hopes that the water highway to the sea will prove possible. If so, the Volta lake will become an attraction for tourists from many countries.

How is this vast project to be financed? The total cost will be £67½ million. Arrangements have been made with the International Bank for Reconstruction and Development, the Development Loan Fund of the USA, the British Government and the Export and Import Bank of Washington for loans of £30 million. It is hoped that the American Government will also make a loan for the national transmission of electrical power. The Ghana Government will contribute £35 million from its own development fund. It is estimated that returns from the project will be such that not only will the loans be repaid and the scheme become fully self-liquidating over a period of fifty years, but a fund will also be established for future development.

Linked with the Volta project will be a group of American aluminium companies to be known as VAICO, which will finance the construction of a smelter, at a cost of £100 million, using 300,000 kilowatts of power continuously and paying nearly £2½ million annually to the Volta River Authority for electricity. The company will at the first stage import bauxite to smelt; later it is planned to use the raw bauxite which awaits utilisation in Ghana. This will involve not only a vast productive enterprise, but the building of towns, railways, roads and a special harbour by the government. This vast scheme was included in the first Volta River project, but has been postponed because of its cost.

How far can the Volta project be described as socialist? It was initiated not by private enterprise but by the government. It was a part of a state plan for Ghana's patterned construction. Its origin therefore was essentially socialist. The project itself will be partly public enterprise, partly private enterprise. The power development will be undertaken from public resources, while the development of the smelter will be by private enterprise. But the balance is undoubtedly on the side of public enterprise—the dam, the power station, the man-made lake, the water highway, the distribution of electricity throughout Ghana's industrial sector. The smelter is essential to the scheme and will make a vital contribution to its economic stability by purchasing electrical power at commercial rates, but it is an appendage, not its body. The Volta project is a socialist arterial highway with a capitalist feeder.

The fact must be faced, however, that the new industries which it is hoped to attract by the provision of electrical power will add significantly to the private sector in Ghana's economy. It was Aneurin Bevan who said that socialism is the science of priorities. Ghana has depended in the past and, indeed, depends at present mainly on its cocoa and its agriculture. They are being brought under co-operative plus state control as already described.

The next stage is to increase wealth production by industrialisation. To make this possible there must be electrical power. The Volta scheme therefore became a priority. But how to industrialise? Following its Volta and other commitments Ghana has not the accumulated capital to establish new industries on a large scale or even to pay interest on large loans. It has not the technicians to take responsibility. Therefore, in the first stage of national construction the new industries must be in private hands, and in practice this stage must be for a considerable period; the capitalists will not come without such a guarantee. But, meanwhile, Ghanaians will be learning the techniques of skilled work and management. They will be ready to take over when the time comes.

In this summary of priorities I have omitted one project which came before the Volta scheme and is almost as impressive. A key drawback in the development of Ghana has been that no sea-going vessel could dock at Accra. Goods and passengers had to be transferred to boats some distance from land and rowed through the surf to the dock.

President Nkrumah, when he came to power, set in motion a large plan to construct at Tema, eighteen miles from Accra, at a cost of £18 million, a modern deep-water port providing berths capable of handling up to two million tons a year. I saw this project during construction, the long arm built of huge boulders brought down from the hilly country, the great curve of stone along the front, the fishing harbour adjacent to the port, Tema New Town for the dock workers, Tema New Village for the fishermen and their families. The eventual population is estimated at 100,000.

It was an inspiring experience. Here was socialist construction such as I had not seen anywhere in Africa south of the Sahara. Every part of this—docks, railways, towns, with their incidental schools and hospitals—is a publicly-owned service.

Such is the basic economic structure of Ghana, the beginning of socialism, plans for socialist fulfilment. But socialism is not only planning under public ownership. It is the fullest possible use of the nation's resources for human development: education, health, housing, and security in old age and against the unhappy interruptions of normal life—sickness, injuries, unemployment. What of the social services of Ghana?

The old colonialist government appointed a commission on education. More was achieved in the five years from 1951 to 1956 than the commission believed possible in twenty years. In 1951 an 'accelerated development plan' was introduced. Fees for primary schooling were abolished and big school-building and teacher-training programmes begun. As a result, the number of primary schools grew from 1,081 to 33,120 by 1956, the number of middle schools nearly doubled, and the number of children in these two types of junior schools went up from 204,000 to over 545,000. It is easy to write and read these figures: not so easy to appreciate the concentration and devotion of effort which they represent.

Emphasis is now being placed on secondary and technical education to enable Ghanaians to perform all the tasks of administration, of the professions and of the skilled research, managements and crafts, which their Africanisation demands. In 1950 there were only 2,776 pupils enrolled in secondary schools. In 1959, 11,111. In 1950 there were as few as 266 enrolments in government technical and trade institutions; in 1959, there were 2,782.

In addition, there is provision for specialised study and advanced education. There are, for example, a Law School and a College of Business Administration. But most important are the University College of Ghana at Legon overlooking Accra and the Kwame Nkrumah University College at Kumasi. The Accra College, completed in 1960, has 1,174 students in residence, taking the arts and science degrees of London University. In addition, it organises extra-mural studies. Consider the significance of these figures: in 1951 six degrees were awarded by the University of London to students in Ghana; in 1959 the number was 77.

The university at Kumasi began as a technical college, with departments covering agriculture, commerce, estate management, engineering, science, pharmacy, architecture, building. Like the university at Legon, its students qualify by London University examinations. The status of the college has now advanced to a university.

These new Universities have the advantage of the most modern construction and equipment. Educational institutions in different parts of the world seem to rival each other in the donation of books and apparatus. In the summer of 1962 I went round a well-known college in the West of England with an English lecturer at the Kwame Nkrumah University. He told me that the equipment and library at Kumasi were the better of the two. The Ghanaians take great pride in their universities and give a high priority to educational expenditure.

There has been a parallel advance in the provision of health services. There are modern hospitals in the towns and dispensaries for groups of villages. The Central

Hospital at Kumasi and the extended hospital at Korle Bu are as impressive as recently-built hospitals in Britain or America, including special provision for maternity cases and for children. The rural dispensaries are in effect small hospitals with wards for men and women and an operating theatre. They are under the charge of a trained matron, with a doctor serving a number of villages on call. Emphasis is placed on preventive medicine with medical field units, health centres, and health education. Special services are at work to suppress endemic disease such as yaws and trypanosomiasis and there is a comprehensive leprosy service. The greatest difficulty at present is shortage of qualified staff of both doctors and nurses. There is a nurses' training scheme but it was interesting to read in Ghanaian papers in 1962 of an agitation which paralleled the nurses' campaign in Britain for better conditions as the first essential to the enrolment of recruits. The Ghana government now recognises the urgency of the need to train medical and nursing staff.

Visitors to Ghana in the colonialist period—as, indeed, to any part of Africa or Asia—were shocked by the housing conditions of a large part of the population. In Accra the massed primitive shacks with their primitive sanitation were inescapable. When the Queen visited Ghana they were hidden from royal eyes by fences along the main routes (the same thing was done in Lagos at the time of Nigerian independence; indeed, so that we may not be too self-righteous, one has heard of not dissimilar coverings of unseemly sights in England). The tattered slums were breeding grounds for disease.

I remember hearing complaints from Ghanaian trade unionists that the government was building its luxurious Ambassador Hotel for European visitors in 1956 rather than re-housing the people. Certainly one of the strongest impressions in Accra even in years following independence was the contrast between the new and startlingly fascinating architecture of government buildings, embassies, banks, business offices and the homes of the higher income groups with the shambles in which so many of the people lived. The contrast between slums and mansions is to be seen, of course, in London and New York, but not quite so emphatically.

The Ghana government is now, however, tackling the housing problem in a big way. Already 80,000 people have been rehoused on government or corporation housing estates. During the period of self-government before independence a large-scale scheme of home-ownership was begun on the basis of hire-purchase. In 1956 the Gold Coast Housing Corporation was established, and in its first four years it opened new estates all over Ghana and built houses to the value of £61·5 million. Many of these new houses are delightful: bungalows in Accra under a shade of palms, two-storied terraces in Kumasi, more windows than walls as they face the sun.

Mention has already been made of the New Town and the Fishermen's Village at Tema, covering 64 square miles and consisting of seven communities of between 10,000 and 12,000 inhabitants, each with their schools, social centres, churches, shops and dispensaries. Anyone who knew Ghana in the 'fifties will not recognise the Ghana of the end of the 'sixties.

Social welfare signifies something very different in Ghana from its meaning in Britain. It is not so much a matter of benefits distributed by the state as of community self-help. I first saw this during the pre-independence period when self-government was already arousing the spirit of a renaissance. What is now the province of the Social Welfare and Community Development Department was then known as Mass Education. I recollect a small village hall in the distant north where six adults, four men and two women were learning to read and write from a schoolmaster, chalk in hand at a blackboard, giving voluntary service after his school classes were over.

But Mass Education was much more than the acquirement of literacy (although 160,000 adults *have* attained literacy since 1952). I visited a centre where throughout the year thirty or forty villagers spent a week acquiring different kinds of personal and social knowledge. The centre consisted of a row of well-built single apartments round a lawn, a dining room, a hall for lectures and demonstrations. The subject during the week of my visit was hygiene: a doctor instructing forty women. It was like one of the ILP Summer Schools in the 'twenties in its combination of comradeship, serious study and social fun.

Mass Education was still more than this. Villagers deep in the forests were, under instructors, cutting a way through the trees and undergrowth and building feeder roads to the main routes to the towns so that they could exchange their produce for previously unknown goods in the shops and link themselves with the social and cultural development which was sweeping the country. They were building halls and schools, digging trenches for irrigation, organising the collection of refuse, improving sanitation. An extraordinary voluntary co-operation in personal progress and community betterment.

These and other activities have now been co-ordinated in the new Department, which not only embraces mass education and construction in village development projects, but social welfare in all its aspects and special campaigns for health, agriculture and housing. The projects extend from road and school building to water and sewage schemes and to campaigns for the use of insecticides by cocoa farmers and other agriculturists. (In January, 1958, only sixty-six gallons of insecticide were sold. In December, 1959, after seventeen months' campaign, the sales were 43,670 gallons.) The government encourages the wide voluntary service by grants. In 1959, 1,222 projects were completed at a cost of £5,178,000. These activities at the grass roots of the lives of the people reflect the spirit of Ghana's socialism more deeply, I would say, than any other development.

Deservedly, the work of the Social Welfare and Community Development has earned an international reputation, particularly in other countries emerging from colonialism. Characteristically, Ghana is now helping other countries in the field of community development. She has given training to four students from British Guiana and one from the West Indies under a mutual technical assistance agreement with the United Kingdom. The government has provided six scholarships to the Foundation for Mutual Assistance in Africa South of the Sahara; the candidates selected come from Nigeria, Northern Rhodesia, Tanganyika, Ethiopia and British Somaliland. Ghana has been a pioneer. Her example is now being widely followed in the new African states, where the same spirit of community service is to be found.

In 1957 the Ghana government supplemented the local effort of the villages by establishing a national Workers' Brigade of young men and women to perform community service. This was an idea adapted from Israel, originally launched to meet two problems—widespread unemployment, on the one hand and, on the other, the need for development in every social and economic sphere. To train youth and put them to the task was the motive. A civilian army of construction.

The definition of youth was generous. It extended from fifteen to forty-five years of age. But judging from a display which I saw in Accra at the Republic celebrations, the main body of the Brigade are young; they were smart in green shorts and tunics (the skirts also short), and they marched and did their physical jerks with disciplined enthusiasm. There are now 12,000 of them, living in thirty-one camps.

Nkrumah, proud of this growth, chuckled happily as he told me that when he opened the first camp in Accra in November, 1957, it had only forty-five members. I was astonished to learn of the variety of the training and the work done. The boys are apprenticed in masonry, carpentry, plumbing, automobile fitting, electrical engineering, vehicle mechanics and tractor operations. The girls learn farming, including poultry-keeping, the marketing of produce, food preservation, household duties including cooking and serving, and secretarial and office duties.

The Brigade began by constructing feeder roads, small water supplies, such as wells and tanks and minor dams, the erection of schools, clinics and communal halls, drainage schemes, village housing and rural electricity supplies. Now its functions have extended greatly. It has over 10,000 acres of land under cultivation in different parts of the country: rubber, banana, plantain and oil palm plantations in the western region; tobacco, yam, millet and rice in northern Ghana, Ashanti and Brong-Ahafo; poultry and fisheries in the Volta region; and coconut and vegetable gardens in the central region. During the appropriate seasons there are large cultivations of cassava, maize and groundnuts in almost all the camps.

The success in these fields led the government in 1960 to name the Brigade the 'Agricultural Army of Ghana'. It was charged with the duty of conquering the forests for food production. But activities are not being channelled into agriculture only. Perhaps the outstanding achievement is the construction of four-flat houses on the Kwame Nkrumah Estate at Kumasi; they are a showpiece. To mention after this that the Brigade has made pavements in the streets of Accra and Tamale may appear an anti-climax; but it is important to mention that these young constructors also serve as an emergency force on occasions of unexpected need. They did a fine job at Takoradi, Cape Coast, Accra and in many other towns and villages in providing temporary structures for those rendered homeless by floods.

The originators of the Brigade had the idea of transforming the camps eventually into co-operative settlements similar to the egalitarian Kibbutzim in Israel, but it is doubtful if development will be on these lines. The tendency is to mould the Brigade as a disciplined civilian force on an army model. At the beginning the Brigade was placed under the Ministry of Labour, Co-operatives and Social Welfare, with a special Board representing Community Development, the Trades Union Congress, the Farmers' Council and the Ex-Servicemen's Union. But it has now been placed under the Ministry of Defence, although the government is at pains to emphasise that 'while receiving almost military discipline, the organisation remains basically civil and is in sympathy with the daily lives and basic needs of the people.' As evidence of this it is pointed out that the national organiser is a policeman!

Libertarians will see obvious dangers in this tendency, but it is a relief to see a country recruiting its youth not principally in military forces, but into an army devoted entirely to constructive community activity.

President Nkrumah's conception of socialism demands personal service in contrast with personal gain. British newspaper reports have sometimes presented a different image; we have been given the picture of a man who seeks grandeur and ostentation. I visited his home when he was Prime Minister in 1956: a four-foot wall, a wooden gate, a grassy patch, a rough pathway before a large house. There were numberless men, women and children —naked toddlers played on the gravel of the path. Nkrumah occupied only two rooms and a veranda. The other occupants of the house were relatives, who, African-like, had poured in upon him with his success. No Prime Minister I have known lived in such simplicity.

I have been only in the lounge of Flagstaff House, where Nkrumah now lives, comfortable with settees and armchairs, but certainly not luxurious. It has been reported that a costly retreat is being built for him away from Accra. He needs a retreat, but he must have become a changed man if he does not continue to live in personal simplicity. Neither in Ghana nor in London have I ever found him seeking the fleshpots.

I dwell on this because it illustrates Kwame Nkrumah's socialist convictions. When Ghana was approaching self-government, the British government built impressive residences for the new ministers. Prime Minister Nkrumah rejected them on behalf of himself and his colleagues. They would continue to live with the people. In fact, it did not work out like that. Some of the ministers were, within a few years, living in palatial mansions. They could not have afforded to live in such circumstances on their salaries. There were allegations of corruption.

Then Kwame Nkrumah did something which no other head of a state has done. He demanded that each of his ministers should reveal his income and possessions and how they were obtained. He insisted that they should surrender all financial and business interests and live at a reasonable standard. He commanded this as the only conduct consistent with service and socialism. He dismissed ministers who did not conform, though he has since reappointed two of them, partly in recognition of their past service to Ghanaian freedom, partly because of their abilities and influence.

Nevertheless, doubts about the future of Ghana remain in the minds of many who cherish liberty and democracy. Leaders of the Opposition have been arrested and detained for long and indefinite periods without trial or with inadequate defence; others have fled into exile. A one-party state has been set up. Ministers frequently speak in terms which are intolerant of any criticism and threaten dire consequences. The cult of personality, disowned in Russia, goes to extremes in Ghana: Dr Nkrumah is not only President and Prime Minister—he has become 'The Osagyefo', a superman, a Messiah. These tendencies are disturbing even to those who admire Ghana's social achievements.

In part they are a reflection of the stage of Africa's political development, the supreme need to build a sense of nationhood from diverse racial, tribal and religious loyalties. Ghana had this problem particularly in the resistance of the Ashanti and some of the northern peoples to incorporation in a united state. It had to overcome the opposition of powerful chiefs, regarded as the spiritual heads of communities as well as their political masters. Nkrumah inherited the bitter antagonism of the professional and business élite whom he ousted as the directors of the national movement. His comprehensive socialist planning required, in Ghanaian conditions, a high degree of centralised authority.

These obstacles to democracy were undoubtedly accentuated by conspiracies on the part of some of the Opposition leaders, perhaps by some frustrated members of his own party, to overthrow the régime by taking the President's life. I negotiated the agreement with the Ashanti dissentients before independence when they accepted a general election as an alternative to civil war. I have never been in the presence of so much emotional violence as on that occasion, and I have little doubt that some of those who were subsequently held to be guilty of an assassination plot did in fact conspire. I regretted their detention without trial. In reply to my protests it was argued that a trial would have meant the death penalty and that the pressure of public opinion would have made commutation of the sentence difficult.

In the concluding chapter the adoption of a one-party state by Ghana and many new African nations and of other authoritarian practices are discussed, but here it is important that one misconception should be removed. The attacks on the President's life have been interpreted as evidence of unpopularity. No one who knows Ghana would agree. Sir Geoffrey de Freitas, the British High

Commissioner, has said that Kwame Nkrumah's standing with the people is higher than ever. Ghanaians have transferred to him as the head of the nation the role of both political and spiritual leader which before they ascribed to their tribal chiefs.

Those who recognise the great social and national renaissance which is taking place in Ghana will hope that the present stage of authoritarian rule will be temporary and will be followed by that liberty and tolerant democracy without which economic emancipation remains an enslavement of mind and soul. Nkrumah has conquered mountainous difficulties in the service of his people. His last triumph should be to conquer the psychological barriers arising from the welding of conflicting elements into a nation by crowning it with freedom.

5
The Socialism of Nasser

PRESIDENT ABDEL NASSER'S advance toward socialism has been pragmatic. He had no intention of establishing a socialist society when he organised the Free Officers' *coup* in July, 1952. 'We had neither programme nor any preconceived ideas', he has said. He and his colonels were moved to action by the selfish luxury of King Farouk's court, its nepotism, the corruption of the politicians who served it, the inefficiency of the army under its generals and their trafficking in defective arms, and what seemed to the nationalist-minded officers an undue servility to the British.

The only socialist features of the revolution were the appropriation to the public of King Farouk's palaces and parks and the distribution to the peasants of the land owned by the deposed ministers and their hangers-on in Parliament.

Nevertheless, there was the spirit of a revolution. I was in Cairo shortly after President Nasser seized power and the people had the shining eyes of something accomplished—mostly accomplished *for* them but also *by* them to some extent in the support they gave. There is one test of a new self-respect. (I also found it in Barcelona during the Spanish civil war). The taxi-drivers declined to accept tips.

Nasser was not, of course, devoid of knowledge of revolutions. Ever since he took the plunge in 1945 and established secretly the Free Officers' Movement he had read avidly the histories of national struggles: Hungary, Ireland, India. He and his fellow-officers had long discussions in their quarters. 'We were a small band of intimate friends who tried to weld a common purpose and plan out of our general ideals', he has written.* He had studied Marx and Lenin but rejected communism because of its atheism—'impossible to be a good Muslim and a good communist', he says. It is interesting to know that he read Laski and Aneurin Bevan as well as Nehru.

But socialism was incidental to his thought. His obsession was anti-imperialism. He was shocked when in 1942 the British, determined to have a government on which they could rely, sent their ambassador, Sir Miles Lampson, to call on King Farouk with a fleet of tanks. The King must either appoint Britain's nominee, Mustafa Nahas, Prime Minister, or be deposed. Nasser was shattered by humiliation when the King gave way. He resented bitterly the presence of British troops in the Suez Zone. He saw Egypt as a colonial feudal state, with the great landed families as allies of the imperialists.

From the first days of the palace revolution he stood for the emancipation of the peasants. He destroyed the power of the large landlords by setting a maximum landholding of 200 acres and redistributing the surplus among the landless in from two to five-acre plots. He found that this was not enough, and he started on the road which has led many African states towards socialism. He organised co-operatives.

During these early years of the revolution Nasser's mind was developing and changing. Despite his anger against British intervention and occupation, the Revolutionary Council in 1954 declared: 'Egypt to-day stands in all respects with the West'. Seven months later Nasser was aggressively neutralist, saying: 'To us Egyptians, there is no difference between a Western power and an Eastern one'.

Two events led to this transformation. The first was the British-sponsored Baghdad Pact, with headquarters in Iraq, including Persia and Turkey and stretching to

* *Sunday Times*, June 6, 1962.

Pakistan. Probably Nasser was disturbed because Iraq's leadership of the Arab world seemed to be acknowledged; he began to regard its royal ruler much as he had regarded King Farouk, as in league with the imperialists. An incidental factor was the disinclination of the Western Powers to provide Egypt with arms, although they supplied Israel. But the greatest factor in changing Nasser's attitude to the West, in making him a neutralist and directing him towards socialism, was the Bandung conference in April, 1955.

The Bandung conference was broadly representative of Asian and African nations. The majority, led by Nehru, were already neutralist, but communist China was also represented by Chou En-lai and there were some American-influenced Asian states there. For the first time Nasser realised the potential power of the Afro-Asian bloc and he determined that Egypt should play a leading part in it.

He was also impressed by the dynamism of the Chinese revolution, though his distaste for communism remained (this did not prevent him sounding Chou En-lai for the arms which the West would not send). He listened to delegates who insisted, more in lounge and bedroom discussions than in speeches, that capitalism was the parent of imperialism and that the aim of the liberated nations should be socialism. He heard this argument from neutralists as well as from China. He returned to Cairo with the declaration that Egypt would stand with Nehru 'both in the international and national fields, the political and the social fields'.

It would be too much to say that Bandung determined Nasser on his subsequent socialist course, but it brought him into a climate of both neutralist and socialist purpose. When he finally decided for socialism he gave himself to its achievement far more challengingly than Nehru. It was the withdrawal of Western financial aid for the Aswan Dam which projected him decisively.

To Nasser the Aswan Dam was a dedicated purpose just as the Volta project was to Nkrumah. It would add one-third to the fertile land of Egypt; it would provide a livelihood for hundreds of thousands of peasants. America was to finance it with British help. America withdrew because Nasser had accepted arms from the communist countries, and Britain followed suit. Negotiations with the International Bank were ruptured. Nasser's beloved plan seemed doomed.

Then, on June 26, 1956, he startled the world, and stunned Britain and France, the owners, by announcing the nationalisation of the Suez Canal. From its revenue he would begin the fund to continue the Aswan Dam project. Britain and France, following military action by Israel, invaded Egypt. Russia threatened war against them. The United Nations denounced the aggression. The British and French troops withdrew. The humiliation of the century.

There were prophesies that the technical management of the canal would collapse when Britain and France withdrew their pilots. It didn't. Egyptian pilots worked long hours while others were trained. In 1960 Nasser reached agreement with Russia for a loan to complete the construction of the Aswan Dam.

By now Nasser was openly avowing his socialist purpose. In July, 1961, Egypt's revolutionary government published a series of decrees giving it effective control of the major industrial and financial concerns. In 1958 Syria had joined Egypt to become the United Arab Republic; the decrees nationalised the banks and insurance companies of both countries and took over the leading textile and mining companies. At the same time 300 industrial concerns were required to sell half their shares to the government, a controlling interest was acquired in 95 companies, and all shareholdings valued at more than £10,000 in 158 companies were seized. The railroads and transport, three-quarters of foreign trade and one-quarter of domestic trade were nationalised. Compensation was given in government bonds bearing 4 per cent interest and redeemable in fifteen years.

Simultaneously a beginning was made towards egalitarianism and industrial democracy. No one was allowed to hold more than one directorate. Taxes were stepped up on high incomes, and £5,000 fixed as a maximum income. The boards of companies were required to have two workers' representatives in seven. A national minimum wage was established. Twenty-five per cent of profits were to go to the workers either in money or social services. Help for old age and sickness was attached to industry and agricultural co-operatives. There was to be a seven-hour working day and, in view of heavy unemployment, overtime was prohibited. A novel feature was a decree not allowing anyone to do more than one paid job. The size of land holdings was further restricted from 200 to 100 acres.

'Only the professions, the small workshops, land-holdings up to medium size and the bulk of the distributive trade remain available to restricted private enterprise', wrote David Holden in the *Guardian*. A revolution almost as decisive as Russia's, 44 years earlier, but without the spilling of a drop of blood.

These socialisation measures were resented intensely by the propertied classes, particularly by the economic and military élite in Syria. Their reaction was largely responsible for the rebellion in September, 1961, which broke Syria's association with Egypt. There were some signs of resistance among the disappropriated owning class in Egypt itself. Forty 'reactionaries' were arrested and 167 capitalists had their property confiscated.

The experienced politician and civil servant will not be satisfied with the exploration so far made of the background of the socialist transformation in Egypt. Bandung may have stimulated socialist thinking, the American and British abandonment of the Aswan Dam project may have inspired the nationalisation of the Suez Canal, but the application of socialist principles on the elaborate scale of the July decrees involved administrative planning and operations which could come only from study and experience. The answer to this problem lies partly in Marshal Tito and Yugoslavia.

Nasser and Tito had become friends first as neutralists, then as socialists. The experience of Yugoslavia was invaluable to Nasser. But this should be admitted: while much has been done to carry out President Nasser's plans, he still lacks the administrative staff and sufficient basic organisation to carry out his ideas in anything like fullness. Much is still a blue-print rather than an achievement.

Indeed there was evidence in the National Budget for 1962–3 that a major share of industry and commerce (particularly when owned by Egyptians) remained in private hands.*

Committed to his socialist course, Nasser realised the need to base the revolution on broad support. In February, 1962, he called together a National Congress of Popular Forces. In a six-hour speech he presented a National Charter which embodied both the principles of Arab socialism and a socialist plan. He made clear the differences between Marxist-Leninism and Arab socialism. Arab socialism, wedded to the faith of Islam, believed in God while Marxist-Leninism denied religion. More immediate in approach and policy was his repudiation of 'the dictatorship of the proletariat'. Egyptian socialism, said Nasser, strove for a régime which would include not only workers and peasants (to whom he promised 50 per cent representation in all state institutions, including Parliament) but representatives of 'non-exploitive capital'. Also, Arab socialism rejected the nationalisation of land. Nasser accepted private ownership of farms, co-ordinated

* See *Socialism in Egypt* by Avraham Ben-Tzur, *New Outlook*, June 1963.

in producers' co-operatives. Finally, he hoped to disarm the feudalists and exploit the capitalists by peaceful means.

After this introduction one would have expected Nasser, like Senghor and Nyerere, to reject the theory of the class war. The reactionary counter-revolution in Syria convinced him, however, that it is 'impossible to neglect the existence of the class struggle'. He gave the warning that, if 'reaction does not disarm itself freely, there will be no alternative to conflict'. Nevertheless, despite the drastic socialistic measures adopted, Nasser did not expect the classless society to be established speedily. The removal of all class distinctions might perhaps take a decade to complete.

The UAR plan is based on a mixed economy, but with power unmistakably in public hands. The dominant public sector will comprise 80 per cent of the economy, the subservient private sector 20 per cent. The target of the plan is to double the national income every ten years. The problem of the excessive growth of population is faced by Nasser and, unlike some Arab and African countries, the need for birth control and family planning is recognised. The increased national income will be used first to lift the standard of living of the workers and peasants.

There is a long section in the National Charter on 'Socialism on the Land'. Co-operation is to be reinforced at all stages of production. While the peasants own their holdings, irrigation and drainage are public services. Nasser's outline of the co-operative scheme deserves quotation:

'True agricultural co-operation is not only the simple credit provision that it meant only a short while ago. Agricultural co-operation has a wide field of activity. It begins with the harvesting of agricultural produce, great success of which has been proven by experience; it finances agriculture and defends the peasant by freeing him from the usurer and middleman who take the great part of the fruits of his toil; it helps him use the most modern tools and methods in order to increase production. After that, it also helps him in marketing his produce, making it possible for him to obtain a fair profit for his labour.'

At the same time the National Charter insists upon the importance of industry, 'the strong foundation of national existence'. Some compensation for Egypt's past backwardness is seen in the up-to-date equipment of its new factories. There is an interesting passage in the Charter on the role of the trade union within socialised industry.

'The worker is the lord of the machine, not a cog in the production mechanism. He is guaranteed an appropriate wage, participation in management and the profits of production, a seven-hour day. Parallel with these revolutionary changes in rights there must also be a revolutionary change in responsibilities. The responsibility for caring for the machines, working them at full capacity and safely, falls upon the workers.

'This new situation has not done away with the tasks fulfilled by the workers' organisations, but instead makes them more important and wider. They can play their leadership role in education towards higher ideological and technical standards. They can continue to guard the rights of the workers, defend their interests, raise their material and cultural levels. They can play a part outside the workshop in the co-operative housing projects, in consumers' co-operation and in the organised utilisation of leisure.'

The 20 per cent private sector of industry is to be strictly controlled. 'In its new role, private capital must recognise that it is subservient to popular authority, the same as public capital,' says Nasser. 'This authority will guide it in accordance with the needs of the people. It can also terminate its activity if it should attempt to exploit or to deviate from the path. The authority is prepared to defend private capital, but its first task is to defend the people.'

There is a valuable analysis in the Charter of the conditions for the acceptance of foreign aid, loans and investments. Priorities are put in this order: (1) unconditional aid (described as a tax on the formerly imperialist countries for the benefit of the countries they once enslaved!); (2) unconditional loans, whose problems end when the capital and the interest are paid; and (3) investment, especially in fields requiring know-how lacking within the nation. The disadvantage of this third method is that it means 'allowing foreign elements to share in the resources of the country and transferring to them part of the profits every year'. But sometimes it is necessary in the interest of specialised techniques. As a matter of fact, one of the contradictions in international economics is the large financial aid the socialist United Arab Republic is now receiving from the capitalist United States of America. The US Care programme is helping to feed four million Egyptian children. Other American relief programmes reach another million people. 'United States Government shipments of surplus wheat supply 50 per cent of the country's wheat consumption,' wrote David Holden in the *Guardian* (December 8, 1962). These surplus shipments are paid for in Egyptian pounds which are then made available to the UAR Government in the form of local credits to finance development projects. 'Arab socialism', as a neutral observer put it to me, 'is getting a pick-a-back from American capitalism'.

No doubt Nasser would say that this provision of aid from America is a tax due in compensation for its betrayal of the Aswan Dam project; it is given unconditionally, and there is no reason why the UAR should not accept it. But the need to do so shows how far the UAR has to go in providing self-sufficiency in order to lift the economic level of the people. America's motive for the aid? Partly humanitarian, no doubt, in seeking a life-saving outlet for her unsaleable stocks of surplus food; but also a corrective to the policy of Foster Dulles who damned a neutralist nation as an enemy. The wiser President Kennedy knows that Russia's assistance to the UAR must be balanced.

Libertarians will be interested in what President Nasser said on the subject of personal freedom. Egypt is often denounced as possessing a dictatorial régime where personal and democratic liberties are suppressed. More than once I have personally urged upon the President that political prisoners should be liberated. 'Freedom is the only way to motivate man to seek progress,' Nasser acknowledged in presenting the National Charter, but as a socialist he sees freedom as more than liberty of thought and speech and writing. It is the liberty of a full stomach, a good home, health, education, work, security in old age. Nasser wants socialism as the best means of ending the poverty which denies human fulfilment. Given economic self-sufficiency, the UAR can proceed to equality of opportunity for all citizens and social equality and fundamental human rights. His listing of these rights was revealing:

1. The right of every citizen to receive medical treatment in such a fashion that treatment and medicines will not be commodities to be bought and sold. It must be an unconditional and guaranteed right of every citizen. (The influence of Aneurin Bevan, for whom Nasser had great respect, is seen here.)
2. The right of every person to study according to his desire and ability.
3. The right of every citizen to work in keeping with his ability and education.

4. The scope of old age and sickness insurance must be broadened. It must serve as a shelter for those who have fulfilled their tasks in the national struggle.
5. The children are the future generation. The working generation must be responsible for supplying them with all the necessities, and for guiding them in the right path.
6. Women must be equal to men and all the factors hindering their freedom must be removed so that they can participate positively in the life of the country.
7. The family is the foundation of society and it must therefore be accorded all its needs so that it can preserve its traditional status in the homeland and participate in society's life and struggle. This will be possible in the society of prosperity and individual freedom.
8. The freedom of faith and religion must be secure in our free new society. The eternal spiritual values derived from religion can guide man and give him limitless possibilities to work for justice, prosperity and fraternity. . . .

It was here that Nasser remarked that freedom is the way to motivate man to seek progress. 'The individual is not free,' he added, 'unless he is liberated from exploitation. This is the fundamental that opens the gates of political freedom to social freedom. The eradication of the differences between the classes and the liquidation of the exploiting elements of the old society will make it possible to establish a democratic life which will bring society as a whole nearer to true freedom.'

There is evidence of a desire in Cairo to find a way of adding democracy to its socialist planning. The *coup* by the officers in 1952 was the work of a small group. It was carried out in the interests of the people but not by the people. One of its first acts was to destroy the elected

Parliament because it was the creature of corrupt exploiting lords of the land. For a time the Council of the Revolution made no pretence of seeking the endorsement of a popular vote. It detained political opponents. Its decrees were law. But Nasser saw at an early stage that if his revolution were to stand it must be based upon the popular will and have popular sanction. He experimented with means progressively to realise this.

He began by forming the 'Liberation Front', an amorphous body which served little purpose except to arouse mass approval of the revolution. Processions and demonstrations were staged, reflecting emotional enthusiasm. The workers and students in the towns genuinely responded; the peasants were stirred to interest as they obtained land; influential Egyptians climbed on to the bandwagon to prove their loyalty to the new régime. The 'Liberation Front' had no executive power. It served as a cheer-leader.

Five years after the *coup* Nasser set up something in the nature of a Parliament and established the 'National Union' to be the instrument of election. The Union was not a political party so much as a broad expression of national unity behind the revolution. At the roots, its groups were popularly elected, but as the pyramid rose there was selection of the candidates and half the final Assembly was appointed. The Union had no programme or aims beyond the assertion of Egypt as a nation and its renaissance. It was a coalition of all classes. Before long, different groups within the Union manœuvred for their own interests and aims. Wealthy reactionaries sought to use their social influence and business or administrative experience to defend their privileges. Communists who had escaped imprisonment tried to convert it into a 'National Front' of legalised parties, both Left and Right, with the intention of ultimately capturing it. Social Democrats wanted to transform the national coalition and its Assembly into a Western-style legislature.

The Union gave some semblance of democracy to Egypt and served perhaps as a stepping stone, but when Nasser moved forward from national revolution to socialism it was quite inadequate. He has said frankly that the Assembly would not have endorsed his socialist decrees of July, 1961, and consequently he ignored it. The economic revolution was announced without reference to the deputies. Subsequent events showed, indeed, that the reactionaries had come out on top in the National Union. Some of its leaders led the conspiracy which severed Syria from Cairo because of the programme of socialisation which he announced. The National Union and its Assembly were dissolved.

A third experiment towards democracy has now been initiated: the 'Socialist Arab Union'. President Nasser takes this very seriously; he cancelled his attendance at the Casablanca Group of African States in order to campaign actively for the new Union. Unlike its predecessor, the SAU has a definite aim: UAR socialism first, expanding to Arab socialism. How far the Union will prove to be an instrument of real democracy remains to be seen. It was initiated from above. The Executive consists of Nasser's officer colleagues with some civilian associates. They have laid down conditions of membership which exclude non-socialists—and even declared socialists of doubtful background—from control. The members of the Founding Committees throughout Egypt have been selected from, or at least endorsed by, these leaders, and it is from this membership that the people appoint the district executives. These elected members form the Provincial Congresses of the Socialist Arab Union, who in turn elect the Central authority. Fifty per cent of the Provincial Congresses and the central authority must be workers and peasants.

This is not formal democracy. The most that can be said is that President Nasser is endeavouring to inspire the new constitution with a democratic dynamism. He is endeavouring to arouse the lively co-operation of the peasants, the workers, the common people. It approximates to a one-party system more closely than the previous National Union because reactionaries who oppose socialisation are excluded from nomination and election. But Nasser knows that if co-operativisation of agriculture and socialisation of industry are to succeed he must gain the active goodwill and co-operation of the peasants and workers at grass roots and factory bench. That is his aim.

One's doubt about President Nasser's policy is that he is not prepared to accept the verdict of an 'illiterate peasantry' in free elections. The major parties in other African states do so, confident, with reason, that the people will support candidates who stand for national emancipation and social justice. It is unlikely that President Nasser's Arab Socialist Union would suffer defeat anywhere if opponents were free to nominate candidates against it. He has no reason now to withhold complete democracy from the people.

The aim of doubling the national income within ten years involves industrialisation to expand wealth production, but here the UAR planners have faced an even more urgent problem. The population was growing so fast that starvation threatened unless food supplies were increased. Before the 1950s Egypt had to import food to maintain even the low standard of life which her people had to endure. Hence priority had to be given to agriculture, first through extending the area of cultivated land by reclaiming the desert and the waste land; second, by increasing the productivity of the cultivated land by modern methods of agriculture, the use of fertilisers and of new seeds; and, third, by the introduction of a balanced economy into the countryside through the creation of light industries.

Hence the emphasis on the Aswan Dam and the one million new acres of fertile land it will make available. But the Aswan Dam is not alone. There is an even more fruitful project in what is happily called the New Valley, running parallel to the Nile—a string of oases in the low-lying land of the Qattara Depression. Here subterranean waters are being lifted and channelled and it is hoped actually to open out eight million acres of cultivatable land. The project is breathtaking in scope.

Hence the new factory at Kima, near Aswan, which is already producing 1,200 tons of fertilisers a day. Hence the use of the co-operatives to encourage the use of new methods of agriculture and of new seeds and mechanisation. Hence a beginning in the construction of village factories, a revolution in the village pattern and experience, to provide household amenities never before known.

This does not mean an absence of larger scale industrial expansion. The Aswan Dam—'a project greater than the building of the pyramids 5,000 years ago'—involves the labour of 18,000 men, working with Russian equipment under the guidance of Russian technicians. (How stupid America and Britain were to withdraw!) The construction will not be finished until 1970 at least. It will cost £306 million; it will have twelve turbine units and will generate ten billion kilowatts of hydro-electric power a year.

The reconstruction of the Suez Canal similarly involves immense labour. The canal is being deepened and widened so that two-way traffic will be possible. Port Said harbour is being improved and the pilotage system made more efficient. How silly now appear all the prophecies of the collapse of the canal service when it was dramatically nationalised! Its service to world shipping (except, alas, Israel's) is better than it has ever been.

One has only to see Cairo—its vast airport (the junction for three continents), the impressive Nile-Hilton Hotel (half government-owned), the parks, the shops, the mounting blocks of flats—to realise that this is the modern capital of a modernising country. In the background old industries are being improved, new industries established. There is the notable development of the pioneer steelworks at Helwan, the iron ore mines, the textile mills, factories for glassware, electrical equipment, light metals, domestic consumer goods. A Ministry of Industry was set up in 1956 and is working on a five-year plan.

How far has the revolution succeeded in raising the standard of life of the people? More so than in any other country in Africa; indeed the progress made during the last ten years is probably comparable with any in the world. In 1952–53 the national income was £228 million. By 1960–61 it had become £1,397 million and in 1961–62 it is expected to reach £1,556 million. The peasants and workers have been allotted the first priority in this advance by the redistribution of land and the establishment of the minimum wage and a share of industrial profits. Education has advanced from less than 40 per cent of the school-age population in 1952 to 78 per cent to-day. The 100 per cent target is expected to be reached in the second decade of the revolution. The progress in secondary, technical and university education has been similar.

If anything, the advance in the health services has been even greater. In the early 1950s nearly all the rural population were infected by endemic diseases. I can write from personal experience. In 1950, on my first visit to Egypt, I was horrified and repelled by the appearance of the children in the villages. Almost every boy and girl had festering sores around the eyes. Ophthalmic diseases were accepted as a part of life. In 1960, when I again visited Egypt, it was rare to see such a child; a medical campaign against the infection had been carried out and a hygiene campaign against its causes. This had been done largely by the setting up of rural social units, which provide for medical treatment of out-patients and the eradication of endemic diseases, supplemented by maternal and child welfare and what is termed 'environmental and health culture'.

These social units are still inadequate because of lack of doctors and nurses, but over 100 have been established, each serving 10,000 people. In the towns new hospitals have been built with transport facilities from the villages. There is concentration on training doctors and nurses. The health administrators claim that 'since the revolution, campaigns against the worst scourges have been conducted on an enormous scale'. It is a justified claim. There is real dedication to the purpose.

Life is becoming fuller and gayer for more and more people. In the towns, sport and athletics have become a rage, with the Cairo stadium packed, and even in the remote villages one sees football posts. Television was established only in 1960, but already there is a network of transmitters with five main stations and eight satellite stations. The fact that 200,000 television sets have been installed is an indication of the higher economic level of a large part of the population.

It is significant that President Nasser has named his new mass electoral organisation the Arab Socialist Union and that he retains the national title, the United Arab Republic. He is thinking in terms of the federation of all the Arab nations spanning the north coast of Africa as well as of the Arab states of the Middle East. Egypt has from the first belonged to the Arab League linking the independent Arab nations, but since the UAR moved towards a socialist pattern it has challenged the feudalist régimes of the less advanced states and encouraged the revolutionary movements against them.

In the spring of 1963 came the revolution in Iraq against the Kassem régime which had betrayed the earlier revolution of 1958, followed by a parallel revolution in Syria. They were led by the Ba' ath socialists with whom Nasser had quarrelled in Egypt, but nevertheless an agreement was at first reached to federate the three territories.

This unity has since been broken and it remains to be seen if it can be restored.

President Nasser is confident that the revolution against the old order of monarchs and sheiks and Imams will extend to other Arab countries. He had already seen it break through in the Yemen in almost exactly the same pattern as in Egypt; indeed, it largely took place under his tuition and by his military aid. He has seen the successful war for independence in Algeria, and, more than that, the socialist revolution which Ben Bella has inaugurated. He is aware of the socialist Opposition in Morocco, the socialist objective of the government in Tunisia (moderate though it be), the revolutionary movements in Saudi-Arabia and Jordan. He has no doubt that they will triumph, though Arab unity is still distant.

The one cloud in President Nasser's dream of this greater union is Israel. He is obsessed by this penetration of his Arab continent by the Jewish state. The Arabs had reason to resent the manner in which the Jewish National Home was initiated. There was duplicity on the part of the British government, which desired the co-operation of both Arabs and Jews in the First World War. When the mandate was withdrawn, the Jews announced the state of Israel, drove out a million Arabs in the war which followed, and ever since the Arabs have huddled as refugees on the frontier. The aid which the American and European Jewish communities have poured into Israel has led President Nasser to regard it as a bastion of Western imperialism.

This is a book on African socialism, but Israeli socialism cannot be separated from it. Israel is perhaps to a greater degree than any country a democratic socialist state. Its population has done heroic things in creating a modern society from desert and swamps, and this has had a great influence on Africa. African leaders have gone to Israel both from the new African states and from the national movements which are still to become the governments of emerging states. They have been deeply impressed. They have studied Israeli methods and accepted them as a model for their own countries. In Tel Aviv there is a large wing of the university occupied by African students. More than that, Israeli technicians and advisers have been invited to the new African nations, not least to Ghana, and with devotion have given themselves to the task of aiding in socialist construction. Very often Israeli patterns have been followed.

This has presented a problem to President Nasser because he regards Egypt as African as well as belonging to the Middle East. He has given refuge in Cairo to exiled African leaders, providing them with offices and flats. He has given spacious headquarters to the Afro-Asian solidarity movement. He has welcomed in Cairo the All-African Peoples' Conference, representing the major national movements of the continent; in Cairo also was held the conference of African states to elaborate an all-African economic plan to meet the effects of the European Common Market. The United Arab Republic is associated with the Addis Ababa union of the thirty-two African states. President Nasser is eager to give an African image, indeed African leadership, to the United Arab Republic. In the distance he sees the hope of an association of the Middle East and Africa as a new socialist, neutralist Power-force in the world.

Differences about Israel have caused considerable discussion at African conferences. The United Arab Republic, supported by other North African Arab states, has succeeded in getting critical resolutions adopted, but they have usually been modified considerably and have occupied an inconspicuous place in the proceedings. African influence is likely to be exerted increasingly towards a moderation of the UAR attitude to Israel.

One may hope also that the concentration of the UAR on the tasks of socialist revolution and the preoccupation of other Arab states with their internal revolutionary struggles may lead to a diversion of attention from Israel. It is noteworthy that in his six-hour speech on the National Charter, which covered the problems of Arab unity and foreign policy as well as internal economic construction, President Nasser devoted only three sentences to Israel, and they were defensive rather than aggressive:

'Imperialist plots caused the Arab land in Palestine to be robbed without any right of law in order to establish a military fascism living on war-like threats. The danger lies in Israel's very existence as a tool of imperialism. Egypt is the only Arab country able to bear the responsibility of establishing a national army to guard against the Zionist aggressive imperialist plans.'

If the hostility between the UAR and Israel is to be resolved, much will be demanded of Israel as well as the UAR. The champions of Israel have said that the antagonism of the Arab countries was due to the fear of the ruling monarchs and sheiks that socialism would spread to their territories and peoples. Socialism is spreading. The people of Israel should now prove their socialist sincerity by identifying themselves with the Arab revolution and aiding it by every means. If Israel wishes to win a secure place in the Middle East, it should prove its solidarity with the socialist forces which are creating the future order of the Middle East.

This policy would also undermine the UAR charge that Israel is the tool of Western imperialism. This will be the acid test for Israeli socialism. Is it more pro-socialist than pro-West and anti-Arab? Israel must think of its future as belonging to a Middle East which will be neutralist and socialist. It should hail now the prospect of a Socialist Federation of the Middle East. It should break from the West, resist an alliance with Russia, embrace the non-alignment of the Middle East to which it belongs. If Israel did these things, an accord with the UAR and the Arab states should be attainable.

There is one final thing to be said on this subject. President Nasser is objective, pragmatic, realistic. He began his régime as pro-West. He became neutralist. He began his régime without any socialist purpose. Socialism is now his great purpose. He denounces Israel. He is formally at war with Israel. But he is adaptable. If Israel identified itself with Arab socialism there would be common ground for accommodation.

As I conclude this chapter I am conscious that I have written with growing appreciation. That reflects my study. I began with a prejudice against President Nasser. I had come into conflict with him because of his imprisonment of political opponents without trial. I still deplore the dictatorial record of his régime. I deplore his antagonism to Israel. But as I have done research and seen for myself in Egypt itself, I have become more and more convinced that President Nasser is one of the most creative figures for socialism in our time, of influence not only in the United Arab Republic, but throughout the Arab world, throughout Africa, and therefore of immense significance to all of us.

When Nasser seized power Egypt was a subject country, subject to foreign domination, subject to a monarchy and feudal lords who lived in luxury on the labour of masses of peasants to whose misery they were indifferent. Nasser's 'revolutionary command was the first wholly Egyptian Government to rule the country for over 2,000 years', wrote H. A. R. Philby in the *Observer* (July 22, 1962) on the tenth anniversary of the revolution. 'Some of the preceding dynasties had become at least partly Egyptianised. But the masses had held themselves aloof from government, regarding it as something alien, acquisitive and often cruel.'

President Nasser and his colleagues acted to end alien rule at home and economic dependence on foreign countries. They saw 'the political and economic servitudes in an organic embrace at the root of all their evils'. They threw out foreign influence and began to build a versatile economy able to stand on its own. Then they saw that if the economy was to be really the servant of the Egyptian nation—of the *people*—if the masses were to be lifted from their poverty, it must be owned by the nation. Only then would the nation become identified with the government, with the administration. Only with socialism could a living democracy be established.

It is clear to me that European socialists, perhaps also the socialists of the communist countries, must make a new appraisal of the significance of President Nasser and the United Arab Republic. They are of profound importance to the future of socialism.

6

Will Africa Turn to Communism?

THE developing pattern of African socialism in its present stage has become broadly clear as we have travelled from country to country. It is based on the co-operativisation of agriculture, sometimes supplemented by the collectivisation of the larger plantations; a network of publicly-initiated village industries; state initiative and ownership of impressive national projects for irrigation, generation of electrical power, dockyards and transport; some public participation in the ownership of private industries and their incorporation in overall economic plans—all this accompanied by the enthusiastic expansion of education, health and housing and the dedicated service in construction of co-ordinated groups of armies of voluntary workers.

The governments of the territories we have reviewed are concerned naturally in the first instance with the construction of socialist societies within their own frontiers and in terms of their own conditions. Their socialist philosophy has arisen from these conditions. Thus the theory of African socialism expressed in the writings of Julius Nyerere and Léopold Senghor is founded on the evolution of African society in agricultural territories from tribal community living to community living in modern conditions, without the pressure of a conflict with capitalism, without a struggle between a possessing class and a proletariat. The consequence has been the rejection of European 'scientific socialism'.

This theory may, indeed, be justified in Tanganyika, Senegal, Dahomey and other predominantly agricultural economies which are beginning their limited industrialisation without entrenched capitalist power in major enterprises. One hopes it will be true; the achievement of classless societies without preceding class conflicts would be a transformation giving much greater promise of co-operation and unity. Over a large part of Africa the peoples may ironically reap the advantage of historical imperialist policy which has been to starve them of industries in order to obtain agricultural products; the new nations begin afresh. The spirit of Nyerere and Senghor is the spirit of socialism achieved; it will be a human triumph if it becomes also the spirit of the process of socialist achievement.

It is too much to hope, however, that it can become the pattern for all Africa. President Nasser in the United Arab Republic had to concede in 1961 the validity of the theory of the class struggle following the resistance of the possessing class in Syria, backed by the same class in Egypt, to his nationalisation programme. He now sees the whole of the Middle East as a region of the same conflict between, on the one hand, monarchs and sheiks resisting democracy, rich from the ownership of oil rights, and, on the other, the Arab peoples.

It is clear from the experience of many African countries that the evolution from tribal to co-operative communities does not always avoid a clash between the peoples and feudal monarchs, chiefs and landed proprietors clinging to personal power and possessions. Egypt, Ghana and Uganda are examples. Sometimes this evolution takes place without serious conflict; there are chiefs who have so identified themselves with the people in the struggle against colonialism that they have become a part of the democratic wave. Nevertheless, even in agricultural societies there has been an element of the class struggle.

From the socialist angle one reservation must be made about the change from tribal to co-operative communities. Co-operativisation is not necessarily socialism in terms of economic equality or even of co-operation among all those involved. I have a vivid memory of the exploitation by some of the farmers in the Uganda Co-operative Federation of their Belgian Congo immigrant labourers: they were appallingly paid and housed, a pitiable sight in their ragged clothes and primitive existence. These co-operatives were often associations of large-scale farmers concerned to save expenditure by pooled buying, pooled processing and pooled selling. Such an organisation can be for sectional gain rather than community service. It is possible even in such cases to limit the power to exploit by a legal minimum wage, statutory living conditions and a statutory limitation of profits; but the non-socialist relationship of employer to employee would still persist. Only when the humblest worker has an equitable share in the enterprise and its revenue can it truly be called a co-operative and conform to a socialist pattern.

The theory of the orderly evolution of the tribal community into a socialist society ignores the conditions in those African countries where European settlers seized much of the best land, as in Kenya and the Rhodesias. Here some conflict was and is inevitable. Are we to say that the Nyerere–Senghor theory only applies when African society has been unspoiled by European settlement? A disturbing conclusion.

The theory breaks down even more indubitably when challenged by formidable capitalist industrial penetration. How can Africans face the problem of taking over the European and American-owned mines dominating the economies of southern Africa—the Rhodesias, Katanga and the Rand—merely by the evolution of their tribal communities? In the principle of the desired social organisation, certainly; the solution lies in community ownership of the mines and the use of their wealth for the community. But how can this be realised without conflict, a combination of both class conflict and race conflict, when the masses of Africans are land-hungry impoverished labourers, and the owners of the mining companies are European and American investors overseas? The Nyerere–Senghor philosophy ignores this problem, which is the core of the problem of African socialism.

The financiers and capitalists of Europe and America would care little if they were to lose all their possessions on the continent of Africa so long as they retained their mineral wealth. Capitalism in Africa *is* the ownership of its minerals. One cannot think of an Africa which is socialist without the transference of its mineral resources and wealth to the people.

The known mineral wealth of Africa is based on gold, copper, diamonds, with a new importance in uranium, and includes cobalt, tungsten, zinc and silver. Most of the gold is produced in South Africa, yielding profits of over £80 million a year, about a third of its total revenue. The sources of copper are Northern Rhodesia and Katanga; the diamonds come from most of the southern countries as well as from the West and Tanganyika. De Beers have a virtual monoply of diamonds, controlling over 80 per cent of the world sales outside the Soviet bloc; their value is between £90 and £100 million a year. The different mining companies distribute annual dividends which, as previously indicated, rise to 80, 100 and even 200 per cent.

The formidable power of Africa's mineral capitalism is not only its wealth; it is in its united strength. Many of the main companies are associated by interlocking directorates and shareholdings. The mineral resources of Northern Rhodesia, Katanga, the Republic of South Africa and South West Africa are largely owned by a closely-knit cartel whose members also control the railways of Angola and Mozambique which carry their produce to the ports. This is what African socialism is up against in southern Africa.

It goes without saying that the African people must first win political power in southern Africa; that they must gain technical experience if they are to invade the skilled grades of the mining industries and their managements (they will meet resistance here more from the European workers and staffs than from the companies, which would welcome cheaper labour); that from somewhere finance on a vast scale must be accumulated or borrowed to pay compensation to the companies, unless the take-overs occur in revolutionary circumstances. These considerations make the realisation of mineral socialism difficult and perhaps distant; but without it African socialism cannot be completed.

There is another element in this problem which is important in preparing the blue-print of African socialism. The fact that the mineral production and transport communications are controlled by interlocking companies makes this an issue not for one country alone—not for the Rhodesias, Katanga, Angola, South Africa separately; but together. In southern Africa we already have Pan-African capitalism. The efficient transformation should be to Pan-African socialism. There will thus be an economic incentive to union across the frontiers to supplement the ideological political incentive already strong.

* * *

How far is it likely that African socialism will turn to communism? If by this is meant turning to the communist bloc, the likelihood is small. In this, Nyerere and Senghor reflect most of Africa when they acclaim an African socialism distinct from both Soviet communism and European social democracy. Ghana, Guinea, Mali and the UAR have been cited as communist-inclined. These pages have given evidence to the contrary in the cases of Ghana, Guinea and the UAR. The one state which tends to model its socialist plans on communist experience is Mali, and it is following China rather than Russia.

Nyerere has expressed what can be accepted as a representative African view on the conflict between the communist nations and the West. It is worth quoting because it is a view little understood. He had been discussing the division of the world into the two Power blocs, which he describes as the 'capitalist bloc' and the 'socialist bloc'. (It is a defeat for democratic socialists that communist countries are described as 'socialist' even by neutralist socialists). Capitalism, Nyerere writes, went wrong when it divorced wealth from its true purpose of satisfying human needs to the purpose of acquiring personal power. The object of socialism is to banish poverty, to provide for human needs. Then he adds:

'But I believe that the socialist countries themselves, considered as individuals in the larger society of nations, are now committing the same crime which was committed by the capitalists before. . . . Internationally they are engaged in using wealth in exactly the same way now as the capitalist countries are using it—for power and prestige. . . . In other words, socialist wealth now tolerates poverty—which is an even more unforgivable crime.'

No under-developed country can afford to be anything except socialist, insists Nyerere, but:

'Africa must beware of being hypnotised by the lure of old slogans. I have said already that socialism arose to remedy mistakes which capitalism had made. Karl Marx felt there was an inevitable clash between the rich of a society and the poor of that society. In that I believe Karl Marx was right. But today it is the international scene which is going to have a greater impact on the lives of individuals than what is happening within Tanganyika or within Kenya or within Uganda. And when you look at the international scene, you must admit that the world is still divided between the "haves" and the "have-nots".

This division is not a division between capitalists and socialists, or between capitalists and communists; this is a division between the poor countries of the world and the rich countries of the world. I believe, therefore, that the poor countries of the world should be very careful not to allow themselves to be used as the "tools" of any of the rich countries of the world—however much the rich countries may seek to fool them that they are on their side. And don't forget the rich countries of the world today may be found on either side of the division between capitalists and socialist countries.'*

Behind this view is the instinctive African reaction to all external superiority or domination, whether it be political occupation, military pressure, wealth or any contrast in status. Africa is claiming its equality and is prepared to prove by its own effort its right to equality. Africa is poor? Yes, but it will not go cap-in-hand to the rich, not even to 'socialist' riches. There was striking confirmation of this attitude in the election manifesto published by the Kenya African National Union to which reference has already been made.

A more fundamental argument for the presence of communist tendencies in Africa is the authoritarian form of government adopted by many of the new nations. The UAR, the Sudan, Ghana, Guinea, Mali, even Tanganyika illustrate this in varying degrees. Are these nations likely to slip into the communist pattern?

We should recognise that it is too much to expect that African states when they become independent will immediately, or within a brief period of years, become fully-fledged democracies, either in constitution or in spirit. Democracy cannot be imposed; it grows. It is not a matter of periodical votes to elect parliaments and

* *Spearhead*, February, 1962, Dar-es-Salaam.

governments; the essence of democracy is tolerance towards dissentient views, freedom for their expression, the acceptance of political oppositions, the acquiescence by minorities in majority rule, and, generally, the authority of reason, discussion and public opinion. No people attains to this maturity of democratic conduct without a long history of expanding experience. It is a century since the Chartists demanded 'one man, one vote' for the British people, yet we still have deficiencies in our democratic practice.

Colonialism, which is an alien dictatorship, cannot be transformed into a conscious self-governing democracy in a day. Indeed, the practice of colonial governments in their repeated imprisonment and detention without trial of national leaders during the struggle for independence was a disastrous prelude to self-government by its example in repudiating the principles of civil liberty and democracy. Africans did not fail to note that while British leaders were denouncing Ghana the British government was engaged in a repression in Nyasaland which outraged liberty on a far wider scale.

The fact must be faced that in many African countries the democratic constitutions which accompany independence do not reflect the prevailing social development and require some authoritarian limitation if governments are to function. In a large part of Africa the intellectual élite, sons of the universities and modern ideas, who man the governments and administrations, think and live in a different world from many of their people. The masses can be emotionally stirred against alien occupation; they cannot so immediately respond to the practice of reasoned persuasion involved in democracy. A still bigger obstacle to democratic nationhood lies in the diverse tribal elements in the new African states. It has already been emphasised that the colonial territories do not represent natural association of tribes, or even of races. To integrate them into united, democratic nations cannot be achieved in a few years or a decade. Meanwhile, governments will resort to pressures and compulsions.

The alternative to liberal democracy is a totalitarian or authoritarian society. It is a ground for hope that the African governments have avoided the totalitarian model of Nazism and Stalinism. The only independent state in Africa which can be described as totalitarian is the white Republic of South Africa in its conduct towards the coloured races and all who challenge its policy. But a number of the African states are authoritarian, i.e., not compelling all individuals to one regimented thought or behaviour, not thrusting militarisation or forced labour on the people, but directing them, influencing them by patriotic propaganda, establishing one-party régimes, sometimes ennobling their leaders to supermen, limiting the right of criticism and opposition to a degree foreign to liberal socialism. Their governments regard the achievement of independence, the integration to nationhood, and the construction of socialism as a continuing revolution with peoples diverse, sometimes in self-contained communities, with little experience of democracy. Authoritarian methods alone seem adequate.

Thus in Egypt, and, after some effort towards democracy, in Sudan, there was a military *coup* by a revolutionary intelligentsia in uniform taking possession of the political administration. In Ghana and Guinea, and to some extent in Tanganyika and other states, democratic methods were used to gain power by a civilian intelligentsia which felt compelled to resort in different degrees to authoritarian methods. They could do this because they were popular after their courageous leadership in the struggle for independence, successful in their leadership towards a national and economic transformation, skilled in their mass propaganda and their mobilisation of a mass party, and psychologically triumphant in arousing personal devotion to a national figure as a sublimation of traditional devotion to separatist tribal chiefs.

Four features of the authoritarian nations are distasteful to liberal democrats. The first is the one-party state. This is not just a reflection of a desire for dictatorial power. It arises from three pressures: the inheritance of the national movement which preceded independence, the concentration integrating the tribal system into a united state, and the need to have unity in the transformation to the socialist society. Theoretically, and in some cases actually, criticism, argument, new ideas can be expressed within the party. One remembers that the same claim is made for the communist parties in Soviet Russia and communist countries; judgment must depend on how far the party is co-equal with the nation, how far the democracy within it is real, and how far liberty of expression is permitted by those who do not belong to the party.

This last consideration leads to the second feature of democratic doubt. Political opposition in some African states is regarded as an offence and, in extreme cases, may lead to severe punishments, sometimes without trial, or, when trials are permitted, without proper facilities for defence. These criticisms have most frequently been made of Ghana, already discussed in these pages. They might also with justification be made in part in the case of Nigeria. The issue arose when the British parliament had to decide whether Chief Enahoro should be deported to face a political charge in Lagos. No one with knowledge would describe the Nigerian government as tyrannical or its higher courts as biased, but, nevertheless, the chief was likely to suffer a severer penalty than in Britain. The African states in the present stage of transformation reflect the circumstances and psychology of a national emergency; just as in war time political liberties are curtailed in Britain, so in the revolutionary building of a new national entity in Africa political resistance may be regarded as treachery. We must understand; but this does not mean that we should surrender our ideal of liberty by failing to give asylum to political refugees (a contribution to the future pattern of human society beyond Africa) or that we should not exert our influence to widen the bounds of liberty in Africa and to create the stable foundations there on which liberty will grow.

A third cause of uneasiness among libertarians is the limitation of trade union rights and the state control of the co-operative movement. In Tanganyika strikes are forbidden and in other African countries they are suppressed. Ghana is not alone in bringing the co-operatives within the state economy. The restrictions on the trade unions are partly due, as we have seen, to the conviction in agricultural territories that in the smaller sector of urban industries the unions are able to wield a power and gain concessions which are unfair, in terms of the nation's resources, to the much larger peasant population; partly the restrictions are due to the emphasis on the common national effort in constructing a new society; a strike is regarded as sabotage.

The state control of co-operatives similarly reflects the need to establish an integrated and co-ordinated economy. Nevertheless, these invasions of the rights of workers to withhold their labour, and of the voluntary association of producers and consumers, are a surrender to centralised state power which those who regard democracy as coming from the grass roots of society, as something living and dynamic in which the people consciously participate, will deplore. Perhaps they are necessary in the present stage of African development, but one hopes for changes which will make democracy a reality at the level of the workshop and farm.

The fourth ground for disquiet is the deification of individual leaders, the pursuit of the cult of personality to an extravagant degree. This again is a reflection of national dedication and emergency. It happened in Britain with Lloyd George and Winston Churchill during the wars. It always happens during national struggles or revolutions. Sometimes it is necessary to embody in one person the purpose and emotion of a people. Thus it was that Hastings Banda was regarded as a messiah when he returned to Nyasaland to lead its people to freedom. Thus it is in Ghana where Kwame Nkrumah is exalted beyond ordinary mortals. But the dangers are obvious. Few individuals can resist the pressures of personal power. No nation can become really democratic if one individual with constitutional power is enthroned above others. For the sake of Africa, one hopes that this will prove a passing phase and that those who are the victims of exaltation will move towards sharing their prestige and responsibility.

There is in this national hero worship a danger to the unity of Africa and to the realisation of the Pan-African dream which has inspired leaders and movements throughout the darker years. If in each state the leader is regarded as a superman, it will be difficult to reconcile individual prestige with the self-effacing co-operation which the union and federation of states will require. Yet one has reasons for confidence. Azikiwe accepted the postponement of independence for southern Nigeria in order to bring the North into federation. Nyerere was prepared to postpone the independence of Tanganyika to facilitate the East African Federation. Nkrumah's dedication to Pan-Africanism is beyond doubt. The dispute over the roads to unity, between social and economic co-ordination or political amalgamations, will resolve itself by both being pursued.

Conferences of heads of state will progressively implement social and economic co-ordination; in some regions of Africa political federations and unions will proceed. The union of Ghana, Guinea and Mali is at the moment a marriage in principle rather than practice, though Ghana gave Guinea generous aid when France attempted to sabotage her independence; but it will consolidate and extend. The union of Arab states in the Middle East has had a setback; it will come again and will almost certainly expand across north Africa. There is an exciting prospect here of an eventual federation between Africa and western Asia.

The summer of 1963 will live in African history for its demonstration of unity at the Addis Ababa conference. All the thirty-two independent African states participated and they established a permanent council and secretariat to co-ordinate common action in every sphere. Their first concern is to end all colonialism on the continent and apartheid in South Africa, but they are also preparing for closer political and economic co-operation between themselves. At Addis Ababa the difference between the Monrovia and Casablanca groups was bridged. There is little doubt that within this new union of forces the drive will be towards neutralism and socialism.

But the most promising advance towards unity is in the previously British sphere of east and central Africa. Tanganyika, Uganda and Kenya will federate as soon as Kenya is independent. This will be only a beginning. The African movements of all east, central and southern Africa are linked in PAFMECSA (Pan-African Movement of East, Central and Southern Africa) and their goal is federation of this vast area when its territories become democratically free. Within a few years we shall see the East African Federation extending to Zanzibar, Mauritius (an island 2,000 miles away), Somalia, Ethiopia, Nyasaland and Northern Rhodesia; later to Burundi, Rwanda and the Congo, including Katanga; one day to Southern Rhodesia and the High Commission Territories and, following the liberation of the non-white populations, even to Angola, Mozambique, South West Africa and South Africa itself. In its early days this Federation will provide the answer to the dissolution of the more limited white-dominated Federation of the Rhodesias and

Nyasaland. Afterwards it will provide the nucleus of the United States of Africa.

The United States of Africa will be a United Socialist States of Africa. It may be the end of this century before it is achieved, but no survey of the continent can lead to any other conclusion than that the creative forces of Africa are now fashioning both unity and socialism. It will be an African socialism evolved from African conditions, distinctive in pattern and philosophy, but integrally socialist because progressively it will give to the people the wealth they create, equality in everything which makes for human fulfilment, and the fraternity of a co-operating society. How soon it will also embody all that we mean by liberty will depend upon the advance which is made in the coming together of conflicting elements and the sense of security which grows from stable conditions.

Thinking people everywhere must awaken to what is happening in Africa to-day. It is now the most important, fascinating and significant scene of social—and socialist—transformation.

MAP

AFRICA 1963

OVERLEAF

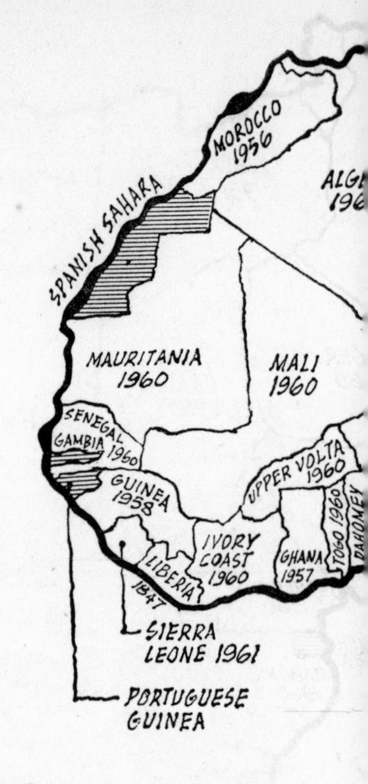

AFRICA 1963

Dates show years when independence was attained

Countries not yet independent are shaded